Cambridge Elements

Elements in Behavioural and Experimental Economics
edited by
Nicolas Jacquemet
University Paris-1 Panthéon Sorbonne and the Paris School of Economics
Olivier L'Haridon
Université de Rennes 1

ADVANCES IN EFFICIENT DESIGN OF EXPERIMENTS IN ECONOMICS

Michał Wiktor Krawczyk
University of Warsaw

John Masson Noble
University of Warsaw

CAMBRIDGE
UNIVERSITY PRESS

CAMBRIDGE
UNIVERSITY PRESS

Shaftesbury Road, Cambridge CB2 8EA, United Kingdom

One Liberty Plaza, 20th Floor, New York, NY 10006, USA

477 Williamstown Road, Port Melbourne, VIC 3207, Australia

314–321, 3rd Floor, Plot 3, Splendor Forum, Jasola District Centre, New Delhi – 110025, India

103 Penang Road, #05–06/07, Visioncrest Commercial, Singapore 238467

Cambridge University Press is part of Cambridge University Press & Assessment, a department of the University of Cambridge.

We share the University's mission to contribute to society through the pursuit of education, learning and research at the highest international levels of excellence.

www.cambridge.org
Information on this title: www.cambridge.org/9781009500357

DOI: 10.1017/9781009263030

When citing this work, please include a reference to the DOI 10.1017/9781009263030

First published 2024

A catalogue record for this publication is available from the British Library.

ISBN 978-1-009-50035-7 Hardback
ISBN 978-1-009-26305-4 Paperback
ISSN 2634-1824 (online)
ISSN 2634-1816 (print)

Advances in Efficient Design of Experiments in Economics

Elements in Behavioural and Experimental Economics

DOI: 10.1017/9781009263030
First published online: December 2024

Michał Wiktor Krawczyk
University of Warsaw

John Masson Noble
University of Warsaw

Author for correspondence: Michał Wiktor Krawczyk, mkrawczyk@wne.uw.edu.pl

Abstract: Amidst concerns about replicability but also thanks to the professionalisation of labs, the rise of pre-registration, the switch to online experiments, and enhanced computational power, experimental economics is undergoing rapid changes. They all call for efficient designs and data analysis – that is, they require that, given the constraints on participants' time, experiments provide information that is as rich as possible. In this Element the authors explore some ways in which this goal may be reached.

Keywords: methodology of experiments, choice experiments, adaptive designs in economics, applied Bayesian statistics, optimal designs

MSC Subject classification: 91Bxx (Mathematical Economics) 62Cxx (Statistical Decision Theory) 62Kxx (Design of Statistical Experiments) 62Lxx (Sequential Statistical Methods)

ISBNs: 9781009500357 (HB), 9781009263054 (PB), 9781009263030 (OC)
ISSNs: 2634-1824 (online), 2634-1816 (print)

Contents

1 Introduction and Overview of the Element 1

2 Causality and Random Assignment 3

3 Optimal Designs 18

4 Discrete Choice Experiments 40

5 Adaptive Designs 64

References 85

1 Introduction and Overview of the Element

Most books about experimental economics start with the observation that experiments can contribute to the understanding of economics, despite some early claims to the contrary. They then proceed with a historical account of the rising popularity and prestige of the discipline; these accounts inevitably conclude that experimental economics is well past its infancy. By now, experimental economics is well established as one of the methods of analysis and therefore we do not think its existence needs to be justified. The goal should rather be to make it as useful a tool as possible.

The key to this is to work on the efficiency of design and inference, so that sample sizes achievable within a reasonable budget can provide rich and precise information. In the current practice of experimental economics, both the design and data analysis plans tend to be rather simple; the researcher may decide on a sample size using a rule of thumb, assign half of the subjects to the control group and the other half to the experimental group, run the sessions, and then conduct some non-parametric tests to see if the dependent variable takes significantly different values in the two groups. Simplicity is a virtue and this approach often works reasonably well.

In other cases, though, more sophisticated methods can yield considerable gains in efficiency. Fields with a longer tradition of conducting experiments have developed a number of techniques that could be applied fruitfully in experimental economics as it matures, but to date this has happened only rarely. One example would be optimal designs seeking to maximise information ex ante (e.g. D-optimal designs). They are employed, for example, in discrete choice experiments conducted by environmental economists (Mariel et al. 2021), but they are not commonly known among mainstream experimental economists.

Then there are various innovations within the profession. Adaptive (aka dynamic) designs (such as the non-Bayesian Perny et al. 2016) and several Bayesian approaches: DOSE (Chapman et al. 2018) ADO (Adaptive Design Optimisation) Cavagnaro et al. (2013) and the approach of Toubia et al. (2013), in which previous responses help to determine what stimuli are likely to be most informative about subjects' preferences, have recently been developed but are not widely adopted yet.

The coverage of these topics in leading texts on experimental economics (e.g. Jacquemet and l'Haridon 2018) and experimetrics (Moffatt 2015) remains patchy. Moreover, promising links between them have been largely overlooked.

In this Element, we explore the pros and cons of the simplistic business-as-usual approach to designing economic experiments. We discuss the pervasive problem of small, underpowered experiments. We point out the factors that make it easier to run large-scale experiments involving simultaneous manipulation of several variables. These include professionalisation of laboratories and the rise of online experimentation. The latter also makes researchers try to shorten their experiments because, compared with the lab, it is harder to keep online subjects focused for an extended period of time. It is therefore imperative to improve the efficiency of experiments. We highlight developments facilitating in absentia dynamic adjustments of stimuli. We also discuss changes in experimental practice, such as pre-registration of experiments and peer review of designs (so that a paper may be tentatively accepted for a journal before the data is collected), that encourage very detailed planning of the design and data analysis at the onset of the project.

We identify the benefits of the novel approaches in terms of efficient elicitation of preferences of subjects. Wherever possible, we try to quantify them based on the measures developed in the literature on Bayesian optimal experimental design, using simulations, or reporting existing empirical results.

We explore the additional insight that these innovative methods yield into the process by which preferences arise and crystallise. There is abundant evidence that the behaviour of experimental subjects is inherently noisy and context-specific. As a result, stability of findings across methods and trials is often disappointing.

We also discuss the costs and limitations of deviations from the experimental economist's 'business as usual'. These include subjects' potential confusion about more complex experiments and possible incentive compatibility and deception issues in dynamic designs.

We strived to base the Element on a consistent statistical approach. During the process of writing, the second author switched from an agnostic position in the classical versus Bayesian question to a strongly pro-Bayesian position. The Bayesian approach is clearly intellectually more satisfying; as Lindley points out, all statistics has some ad hoc element and the advantage of the Bayesian approach is that this is all encoded in the prior distribution. Once the prior has been established, the whole analysis follows clear mathematical logic. The main problem with the Bayesian approach is (and always has been) the computational complexity, due to the fact that the integrals do not have closed form; Gibbs samplers and Metropolis–Hastings Markov Chain Monte Carlo techniques are required. While the classical approach presents a computational framework that is usually much quicker, it became clear that Bayesian computations are now manageable, even with limited computational resources. Furthermore, it is very rare in experimental economics that one approaches a problem with a genuine complete lack of any prior information; there is usually information from previous experiments on related issues and, when genuine prior information is incorporated, one can reach conclusions, even with a small quantity of new information. This is most evident in the case of dynamic/adaptive designs, in which Bayesian updating is the mathematical notion of choice.

The Element is structured as follows. In Section 2 we discuss some fundamental issues of experimental design and causal inference. In Section 3 we discuss the principles of optimal design. Section 4 deals with choice experiments, while Section 5 describes advances in adaptive designs.

The target group is researchers interested in running economic experiments. We assume the reader is familiar with basic concepts of the method.

2 Causality and Random Assignment

In this section, we briefly discuss the key characteristics of causality and show how cause and effect can be established using various approaches to sampling and random assignment, covering such issues as between-subject versus within-subject designs.

2.1 What Do You Mean by 'Cause'?

Experiments are often, and for good reasons, portrayed as a gold standard to establish causality. But what does it mean exactly that X causes Y? How can we find out that it does? Perhaps Y causes X. Perhaps it goes both ways. Perhaps another variable affects both. Perhaps it is mere coincidence. The ontological and epistemological issues of causality have long been discussed; see, for example, Brady (2011) or Thye (2014) for a user-friendly introduction for social scientists, Mahoney and Acosta (2021) and Woodward (2016) for a more in-depth review of 'causality as regularity' and 'causality as manipulation' types of theories, respectively. Classic books include Spirtes (2001) and Pearl (2009). Here, we report a small part of this discussion which seems to be most relevant for the design of experiments in social sciences.

The pioneer of the investigation of causality, David Hume, famously chose the game of billiards to illustrate it: 'Here is a billiard ball lying on the table, and another ball moving toward it with rapidity. They strike; and the ball which was formerly at rest now acquires a motion. This is as perfect an instance of the relation of cause and effect as any which we know, either by sensation or reflection.' Indeed, the collision, with no contributing or intermediate factors involved, will always cause the second ball to start rolling. Moreover, the physical mechanism is well understood; we also can easily establish that the second ball remains motionless if nothing strikes it. Social sciences tend to provide us with less-than-perfect instances of cause and effect. Social phenomena tend to be complex and probabilistic and hardly ever have a single cause. In fact, 'everything is related to everything else'. Moreover, the laws proposed to explain social phenomena are often contested and their validity may vary over time and across cultures. Still, the basic principles of defining and identifying causality carry over from the simpler, physical phenomena.

Correlation If A causes B, observing B is more likely if A has been observed, compared to the situation in which A was not observed. Naturally, a similar statement can be made for non-binary variables: if there is a causal link, we expect a correlation – for example, high values of A being systematically accompanied by high values of B. Clearly, this is not a sufficient condition. One of the authors is an avid, if inept, hockey player. The only time he was painfully hit by a puck (actually, twice on the same night!) was just hours after he received one of his Covid-19 vaccine doses. This remarkable correlation did not turn him into a vaccine conspiracy believer. For more examples, try to google for images using 'correlation is not causation' or a similar query to see time series that are very unlikely to be causally linked (say, the number of Ariana Grande's Instagram followers and the number of cases of African swine fever virus) and yet, over a purposefully selected period of time, turn out to be very highly correlated. While we may easily identify such a nonsensical correlation as spurious (and we may remember from econometrics classes that they arise easily between two random walks with a drift), our minds are compelled to see patterns of causal links if they are slightly more plausible.

Worse, correlation is not even *necessary*, in that other factors will often conceal or even reverse the correlation that we would expect, given well-founded claims of a causal link. An example of particular empirical importance is that of the link between price and quantity demanded. As every student of economics knows, demand is (almost always) downward-sloping; consumers will want to buy fewer units of a good if it is more expensive. Dubbed the *law of demand*, it is one of the very few laws of the dismal science that actually hold. But how do we know that it holds? Looking at the correlation between prices and quantities sold is very misleading, even if the demand can always be met (as in markets for digital goods that can be instantly produced and delivered at no cost). The producer, being free to set the price at any level, is expected to react to (anticipated) changes in demand. Thus, the correlation can easily turn out to be positive: the price is relatively high when a large number of consumers are interested in the product.

This confusion between correlation and causation is firmly established in the language. The relation of 'being independent' in a statistical sense is symmetric: when variable *X* is independent of variable *Y*, then variable *Y* is independent of variable *X*. This is clearly not true in the way these terms are normally used. Most people would agree that the weather on any given day does not depend on the way they dress. The only likely exceptions would be the fans of Murphy's law and *Other Reasons Why Things Go Wrong* who would tend to believe that not taking a raincoat makes the rain more likely. As a side note, many of them could perhaps be less inclined to believe that *taking* a raincoat makes the rain *less* likely, although the two statements are logically equivalent. More importantly, for most people it is obvious that the way they dress depends on the (current and forecasted) weather. Again, from a statistical viewpoint, if there is dependence, it goes both ways. Statistical (in)dependence is thus not an intuitive notion; our minds like to think in terms of *causal* links.

Theoretical Plausibility As in the case of Ariana Grande and swine fevers, correlations in pre-existing data may be purely incidental. With a bit of 'luck' it may even be true of a statistically significant experimental treatment effect, especially when many different tests are run; see Abdi et al. (2007) for the discussion of ways to correct for that. Some theories of causality thus emphasise that a cause must be explainable by a 'law-like statement'. This in itself is difficult to define, but the guiding principle is that a purported causal link is much more convincing if it is predicted by a fairly general theory. If it flies in the face of a theory (and intuition), such as the observation that strangers cooperate more than partners in the public goods game (Andreoni 1988) we need to be wary and conduct careful replications.

Counterfactuals and Manipulability The problem in empirical verification of the law of demand mentioned before was that 'high price' regimes tend to systematically differ from 'low price' regimes in other dimensions affecting quantity sold, so comparing said quantity between the two states does not tell us much about the slope of the demand function. The challenge is to imagine 'the most similar world' and determine what the outcome would have been. The main problem is, of course, that this is typically not directly observable.

Any empirical strategy for identifying the causal link between the price and the quantity demanded using existing data thus requires a component of variation in the prices that can be correlated only with the variation in the price via the law of demand. This is often done with the help of instrumental variables. However, the surest, most direct way is to vary the price randomly, thus by conducting an experiment. In fact, manipulability theories of causality stress just that: X causes Y if exogenous manipulation of X, keeping everything else constant, would tend to affect Y. As Holland (1986) quipped in his highly influential paper, there is ‘no causation without manipulation’. One advantage of this approach is that it breaks the symmetry between the variables, which was characteristic of mere measurement of correlation. Cooling the thermometer will not make you less ill, but treating the illness will lower your body temperature.

While experimentalists may be naturally inclined to endorse the manipulability paradigm, philosophers have raised numerous lines of criticism against it, including anthropocentrism and conflation of ontological and epistemological status of causality. From the viewpoint of a practitioner of social sciences, one major difficulty is that many interesting effects involve purported causes that are not manipulable. Women tend to earn less than men, also when controlling for their education, experience, and other measures of social capital. It would seem natural to say that the mere fact of them being women *causes* their lower wages, although the mechanism involved is likely complex. But exogenous manipulation of biological sex, keeping everything else constant, is unthinkable. In the manipulability paradigm, the sex of an individual can thus hardly be the ‘cause’ of anything. Admittedly, measuring such a causal link is highly problematic even for other approaches. Suppose that the differences in wages disappear if we additionally control for height. Can we say there is no effect of biological sex on wages in this labour market? ‘Just try to be a bit taller’ is not a piece of advice likely to cheer up women unhappy about wage inequalities. Perhaps the relevant ‘most similar world’ here for an average-height man involves being an average-height woman, not a rather tall woman. A discussion of the similarly tricky possibility of considering the category of ‘race’ as a causal variable can be found in Holland (2003).

Timing Another key aspect of causal link concerns timing. We expect the effect to follow (rather than precede) the cause. Sometimes, the effect is significantly delayed, which makes it more difficult to find out that there is indeed a link. For example, it took decades to realise that cigarettes are harmful, because the effect accumulates after years of smoking (although the vested interest of tobacco companies was another important factor delaying the conclusion). At the other extreme, when the reaction is immediate, telling the cause from the effect is sometimes not obvious. For example, many people believe that it is possible to detect that someone is watching us. Titchener (1925), who was probably the first to address this superstition scientifically, suggested the belief could be related to the natural tendency to pay attention to movement. When person A (male) turns around, it is fairly likely that person B (female), initially behind person A, will throw a glance at him. This reaction tends to be non-conscious and immediate (‘system 1’), so it might seem to B that it was A who turned *in reaction* to her gaze (although in truth, it was herself glancing at A in reaction to his movement). Likewise, A, seeing that B is looking at him (and not knowing this was not the case just a second ago), may infer that he himself has turned *because* he could sense B's gaze. Clearly, in the case a researcher assigns a non-zero prior probability to the supposition that gaze may be detected, controlled experiments with randomised glances must be conducted and indeed *have* been conducted and some even confirmed such an ability, although, perhaps predictably, the methods are contested (see Marks and Colwell 2000).

Another difficulty concerns expectations. The outcome may come before the cause when the *expectation* of the cause precedes it. Much like a rooster's crowing does not cause the sunrise, a war need not be triggered by a market plunge; rather, a war may affect the markets before the first shot is fired because there are good reasons to *expect* it to be fired.

Not surprisingly, timing is also of crucial importance in the design of experiments. Ideally, we want the outcome measure to be elicited immediately following the experimental manipulation. We know that no systematic difference between the experimental group and the control group should occur prior to the manipulation (and if it does, it likely implies there is a problem in the random treatment assignment procedure or that our preparations to implement the treatment are poorly hidden). Exogenous randomisation also rules out the role of expectations. Even if subjects expect *some* manipulation, they usually do not know its nature and, maybe most importantly, they do not know to which group they will be assigned.

2.2 Counterfactuals and Randomisation Bias

Suppose we have p treatments (one of which may be the 'control', i.e. no treatment); the treatments are labelled $1, \ldots, p$, we give treatment j to experimental unit i, and denote the outcome by $Y_i(j)$. In our experiment, we obtain the result of applying treatment j to unit i, but we would like to infer what the outcome would have been if any of the other treatments had been given; in other words, when we observe $Y_i(j)$, we would like to infer the values of $Y_i(k)$ for all $k \neq j$. This is termed *counterfactual*, since for run i we gave treatment j and we did *not* give any of the other treatments.

We can represent the situation by a causal diagram (Figure 1); the outcome Y is influenced by the treatment T and other causes C, which may influence which treatment is given as well as having a direct influence on the outcome. The treatment variable T takes values in $\{1, \ldots, p\}$. We would like to infer that $Y_i(j)$ (the so-called potential outcome for subject i under treatment

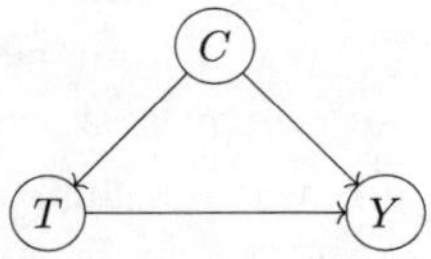

Figure 1 Common cause, treatment, outcome.

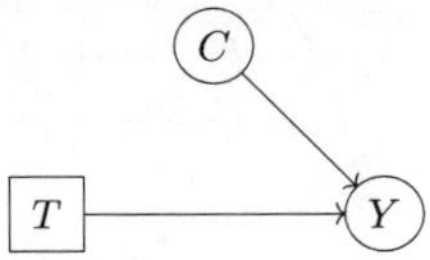

Figure 2 Intervention breaks the link between common cause and treatment.

j – the outcome that would have occurred had subject i been administered treatment j) is independent of T (the treatment actually given), which implies that $\mathbb{E}[Y_i(j)|T = k]$ does not depend on k (and hence that, for each j and k, $\mathbb{E}[Y_i(j)|T = k] = \mathbb{E}[Y_i(j)]$). This is (of course) true if treatments are assigned at random and a *proper* controlled experiment is carried out (i.e. the sample is representative of the population at large and treatments are randomly assigned). This would break the *causal* link between the common causes C and treatment T and result in the causal diagram of Figure 2 (since T is enforced by the experimenter, we denote this by a square node).

Randomisation of treatment means that the choice of treatment is applied irrespective of the values of any hidden covariates that may have a causal effect on both treatment and outcome.

In many situations, though, there are serious obstacles to the construction of a controlled experiment. For example, a sample drawn from college students who *agree* to participate in an experiment may differ in important ways from those who choose not to participate, so the whole sample may be biased. In experimental economics, an important reason for differences is related to the structure of pay-offs. Harrison et al. (2009) hypothesise that the anticipated variance of pay-offs may affect the profile of risk attitudes of the sample of people who sign up to take part. They confirm that announcing a guaranteed show-up fee leads to a relatively risk-averse sample. Therefore, the problem is not whether treatments are assigned in a suitable random manner to a pool of candidates constituting a representative random sample; the *whole sample* of possible candidates may be biased with respect to the prevailing characteristics of the population.

Random assignment may discourage some participants. Levitt and List (2009) point out that in clinical drug trials, it seems much harder to persuade patients to participate in a *randomised controlled* experiment than to persuade them to take a new drug in a non-randomised study. The sample will therefore tend to be skewed for randomised controlled trials.

Framing might matter as well. As pointed out by List (2021), in field experiments, the use of the word 'experiment' itself can cause difficulties, while terminology such as 'trials' and 'pilot studies' may be more acceptable. This applies not only to participants, but also to non-academic partners who are often necessary to run a field experiment. Some of them are prone to respond along the lines of 'we've been in this business for thirty years, we know what to do, and you're telling us to choose something at random?!'

2.3 Randomisation Procedures

At this point, we introduce another important ingredient, which is how to assign treatments to subjects who have agreed to participate. Many procedures have been proposed for the random assignment of participants to treatment groups. We outline common randomisation techniques, including simple randomisation, block randomisation, stratified randomisation, and covariate adaptive randomisation. We describe the methods, giving advantages and disadvantages.

2.3.1 Simple Randomisation

For this, we simply decide how many subjects are to be allocated to each treatment group; if n_i subjects are to be given treatment i, assign i to n_i labels, put all the labels into a hat, and assign them randomly to the subjects. This technique is easy to implement. The disadvantage is that there may be obvious characteristics (e.g. some of the subjects are male while others are female) that lead to heterogeneity; for relatively small experiments, we may find that there are substantially different proportions of men and women receiving different treatments.

2.3.2 Blocking and Stratified Randomisation

A *block*, as explained by Box, Hunter, and Hunter (2005), is a portion of the experimental material (e.g. two shoes on one boy, two seeds in the same pod) that is expected to be more homogeneous than the aggregate (the shoes of all boys, *all* seeds available, not necessarily from the same pod). By confining comparisons to those within blocks, greater precision is usually obtained, because the differences due to belonging to different blocks are eliminated. Blocking seems to have been introduced by Student (1911). It has similarities to so-called *stratified randomisation*. For analysis of data, they are treated similarly; the difference is that the experimenter assigns subjects to blocks, while the strata refer to covariates, or characteristics possessed by the subjects which are observable, but over which the experimenter has no control. For example, the experimenter has control over assignment of subjects to sessions, so that sessions are a natural block; we make sure that the set of subjects in each session can be divided equally among all treatments. The experimenter has no control over whether a subject is male or female; 'male' and 'female' can be considered as strata. In fact, the most typical example in experimental economics of stratification would be by sex; we make sure that we have the same proportion of men treated and untreated as we have for women. Also, we block by *session*, making sure that within each session we have the same number of people in each treatment. For both block designs and stratified randomisation, we would like to ensure that all combinations of levels of the 'nuisance' variables are represented and we would like to make comparisons between the different levels of the treatment variable for each of these combinations.

With stratified randomisation, the researcher identifies specific covariates, where it is understood that there is a potential influence on the dependent variable. Separate blocks are generated for each combination of covariates; subjects are assigned to the appropriate block of covariates. After the subjects have been identified and assigned into blocks, simple randomisation is performed within each block to assign subjects to one of the treatment groups.

Stratified randomisation controls for the possible influence of covariates that could invalidate the research; stratification refers to subjects' characteristics, such as age and sex. For example, consider clinical research where different rehabilitation techniques after surgery are being tested. The age of the subject affects rehabilitation and is therefore a possible confounding variable. With stratified randomisation, we can account for the effect of age.

A block design may make the life of the experimenter more difficult, since we first have to elicit the variables which we want to block. Stratified randomisation is difficult when there are many variables that have to be controlled for. Also, all of the subjects have to be identified *before* being assigned to groups, which is impossible when subjects are enrolled one at a time, on a continuous basis, which is often the case for medical research.

2.3.3 Covariate Adaptive Randomisation

Covariate adaptive randomisation attempts to deal with the problem of not having full details of all subjects by taking into account the values of the covariates of the previous assignments when assigning a new participant to a treatment group, trying to minimise sample size imbalance among the important covariates with each new assignment.

2.3.4 Cluster Randomised Controlled Experiment

A cluster randomised experiment is an experiment in which individuals are divided in groups and the group as a whole is randomised, not the individual; all individuals within a given cluster are assigned to the same treatment.

A cluster randomised experiment is often carried out when *individual* randomisation is not feasible. It can also be considerably more cost- and time-effective when there is extensive existing information about subjects and their treatments and outcomes along with an existing research infrastructure. Compared with individually randomised experiments, cluster randomised experiments are more complicated to design, need more subjects to obtain equivalent statistical power, and require a more complicated analysis (e.g. adjustment for the intra-cluster correlation coefficient of the cluster randomisation). Furthermore, a cluster randomised experiment is usually not blinded, so that external validity may be challenged.

Cluster randomisation may be advisable when spillovers are likely, or when ethical considerations do not permit randomisation at the individual level. This is often the case, for example, with field experiments in the field of education, where randomisation is often at the school or class level.

2.4 Gosset versus Fisher, or Is Artificial Randomisation Really Necessary?

In some settings, comparability of the treatments may be achieved without explicit randomisation. This goes back to balanced designs proposed by Gosset to study the effect of manure on crop yields. The challenge was that the plots into which the field could be divided were not homogeneous. Gosset's contribution is discussed by Ziliak (2014), who challenged some of the findings of Levitt and List (2009). While we prefer to sidestep any controversy, we would like to draw attention to some important conclusions of Ziliak. He compares Gosset's *balanced* designs to *random* designs; for Gosset's experiments studying the effects on crop growth of adding manure, the balanced design demonstrated greater power and efficiency than the randomised design.

In that situation, the field was subdivided into plots. On some plots, manure was added, while other plots were left without manure. The plots were not homogeneous, since the field had ridges of fertility. Letting A denote *control* and B – *treatment* (which indicated that manure was added), Gosset arranged the control / treatments pairwise, so that the design appeared as:

A B B A A B B A
A B B A A B B A
A B B A A B B A

where the ABBA ... layout is in the direction of increasing fertility. The idea was to then take the results *pairwise* and consider the *difference* in crop yields between a control plot A and the *adjacent* treatment plot B.

When there is a positive correlation between adjacent plots, this model presents greater power for estimating the difference in average crop yield between treatment and control. The increased efficiency obtained by using the balanced design can be seen from the following back-of-envelope calculation. Suppose that each observation is the outcome of a *normal* random variable. Let $X_{A,i} - X_{B,i}$ denote the *difference* in treatments for the pair labelled i and there are n pairs. Then $\text{Var}(X_{A,i} - X_{B,i}) = 2\sigma^2(1 - \rho)$ where σ^2 is the variance; $X_{A,i} \sim N(\mu_A, \sigma^2)$ and $X_{B,i} \sim N(\mu_B, \sigma^2)$ and $\rho = \text{Corr}(X, Y)$ where X and Y denote results for adjacent plots. Then, if we have n adjacent pairs, which we may assume independent,

$$\frac{\sum_{i=1}^{n}((X_{A,i} - X_{B,i}) - (\mu_A - \mu_B))}{\sqrt{n}\sqrt{2}\sigma\sqrt{1-\rho}} \sim N(0, 1).$$

Let $s^2 = \frac{1}{n-1}\sum_{i=1}^{n}((X_{A,i} - X_{B,i}) - (\overline{X}_{A,.} - \overline{X}_{B,.}))^2$, then

$$\frac{\sqrt{n}((\overline{X}_{A,.} - \overline{X}_{B,.})) - (\mu_A - \mu_B))}{s} \sim t_{n-1}$$

at least approximately. Since $\mathbb{E}[s^2] = 2\sigma^2(1 - \rho)$, we can see that, taking the observations pairwise and observing the differences, the balanced design is more efficient and powerful than a randomised design when ρ is substantially larger than 0.

Clearly, if the experimental units are known *not* to be homogeneous and the deviation from homogeneity is understood (in Gosset's example, he knew where the ridges of fertility were), then the balanced design enables the confounding effect of fertility ridges to be removed more efficiently than artificial randomisation; we see serious disadvantages to the naive application of artificial randomisation.

The natural analogy in economics is the flow of subjects logging in one by one to an online experiment. Subjects who log in at approximately the same time may have similar characteristics (they come from the same time zone, they have the same employment status, maybe they belong to the same tutorial group, just after class has finished). It may therefore be advisable to assign them to treatments A and B according to the ABBAABBA pattern of Gosset, rather than randomly. This is of special importance when there is some clustering (and the whole group has to be assigned to one treatment).

When the experiment is performed in person, or with online human assistance (so that there is some interaction between the subject and the experimenter), the disadvantage of such predetermined treatment assignment is that it does not allow the experiment to be double-blind. The experimenter may thus inadvertently affect subjects' behaviour. A solution that introduces uncertainty about the next subject's treatment assignment but (almost) guarantees (near) balance is that of *biased coin randomisation* Smith (2014). Hitherto applied in medical trials, it involves treatment assignment which is random, but not independent of previous assignments; the treatment in which the current number of observations is lower has a greater chance to be assigned to the next subject.

2.5 Within-Subject and Between-Subject

The issue of whether to use within-subject or between-subject (or hybrid) designs pervades the design of experiments for economics in a fundamental way. The question is whether to use the *same* subject for repeated runs of the experiment in different treatments (within subject) or to use different subjects for different treatments (between subjects). While within-subject experiments can be more economical, there are disadvantages to using the same subject for several experimental runs; the subject typically has a memory of the previous ones and so repeated runs with the same subject cannot be as independent draws from the same (subject-specific) distribution (The errors will clearly not necessarily be independent and identically distributed (IID) if the subject remembers the previous responses. For example, if the subject is asked *exactly* the same question twice, there may be a random element in the first response; the subject is likely to give exactly the same response the second time through, without thinking again.)

Pricing a Ham Sandwich Charness, Gneezy, and Kuhn (2012) use the following illustrative example in their discussion of relative merits of within-subject and between-subject experiments. A researcher may ask participants how much they would be willing to pay (WTP) for a sandwich:

(a) if they were to buy a sandwich from their neighbourhood bakery, and
(b) if they were to buy it at the airport.

Assuming that the sandwich is identical in both situations and so is actual and anticipated hunger, there is little reason for the WTPs to be any different. Yet people seem to end up willingly overpaying badly at airports, but not in bakeries. Is it just because these are different people or because the food is correctly anticipated to be even worse and pricier during the flight? Or does this discrepancy reveal something about our flawed judgement, whereby €8.95 for a sandwich only seems reasonable in one situation but not in the other?

We can try to disentangle these competing explanations in a controlled study. When doing so, we must decide whether *the same person* answers both questions (within-subject design) or each person only answers one question (between-subject design), one half of the sample being randomly assigned to the question of how much they would pay at the bakery and the other half to the question of what they would pay at the airport. We first discuss some advantages of the within-subject design compared to the between-subject approach and then the other way around.

Advantages of the Within-Subject Design Within-subject design has quite a few important advantages over between-subject design. Firstly, the validity of the analysis does not depend on *random* assignment; both treatments are assigned to the same individual. Obviously, comparing WTPs elicited at an airport to those elicited at a bakery would be worthless, since air travellers are not a random sample of bakery shoppers (or vice versa). A less obvious case is when there is non-trivial and treatment-specific dropout. In contrast to a between-subject design in a within-subject experiment, we can easily restrict our analysis to those who actually made choices in both treatments, thereby distinguishing pure treatment effects from selection effects.

Secondly, for the same reason, within-subject designs can offer a significant increase in statistical power, because there is no noise associated with individual differences. Naturally, as long as the assignment of the treatment is random, causal estimates can be obtained in the between-subject design by comparing the differences in response of the subjects between the various experimental conditions, but the between-subject noise may be substantial. This means that the sample has to be large enough to account for this; if only the sample average is required and σ^2 denotes the between-subject variance, then the sample average variance is $\frac{\sigma^2}{n}$ and n has to be sufficiently large to make this sufficiently small.

For example, suppose we are considering the difference between two treatments and we are in a situation where we can use the same subject for two experimental runs, one for each treatment, and suppose the outcome when treatment j for $j \in \{1, 2\}$ applied to individual i is modelled as:

$$Y_{i,j} = \mu + \alpha_j + \epsilon_{i,j},$$

where $\begin{pmatrix} \epsilon_{i,1} \\ \epsilon_{i,2} \end{pmatrix} \sim N\left(\begin{pmatrix} 0 \\ 0 \end{pmatrix}, \sigma^2 \begin{pmatrix} 1 & \rho \\ \rho & 1 \end{pmatrix}\right)$ and $(\epsilon_{i1}, \epsilon_{i2})'$ are uncorrelated for different subjects. This could arise, for example, if we are considering two different medications for reducing blood pressure, where a subject may have underlying health conditions which affect all treatments in such a way that the within-subject errors are correlated. For such a model, with n subjects $i = 1, \ldots, n$

$$\widehat{\alpha}_2 - \widehat{\alpha}_1 = \overline{Y}_{.2} - \overline{Y}_{.1} \sim N\left(\alpha_2 - \alpha_1, \frac{2\sigma^2(1-\rho)}{n}\right).$$

To get a variance of $\frac{2\sigma^2(1-\rho)}{n}$ from a between-subject experiment, where each subject is used exactly once, we would require $N_B = \frac{2}{1-\rho} N_W$ subjects.

We can see that the reduction in number for an experiment with the same precision (to carry out statistical tests with the same power) is not simply from the fact that the subjects in a between-subject are only used once, but also due to the correlation of the random effects within subjects.

Thirdly, within-subject designs tend to be more efficient in terms of data collection. Typically, the two treatments share a substantial part of the instructions and stimuli. Thus, a decision in Treatment B may be elicited more quickly and easily from a subject who has already made a decision in Treatment A (the subject only has to understand how the two are different) than from a fresh subject, as would have been the case in the between-subject design. This is not an issue in the sandwich example, but it certainly is with more extensive instructions.

Fourthly, within-subject experiments may be more appealing theoretically. For example, if we have a theory predicting the effect of price, we may want to observe actual price change and therefore expose the same agent (rather than two different agents) to two different prices. Likewise, when investigating preference *reversals* (Tversky and Thaler (1990)), we want to observe different choices of the same individuals. The underlying theory often takes the form of some individual utility function. Within-subject designs allow this to be estimated, while between-subject designs generally do not.

Fifthly, within-subject designs yield individual-specific estimates of the treatment effect. This is important if we expect heterogeneity, especially if we want to link these effects with some other behavioural characteristics. Further, within-subject design is the only option if we want to select subjects based on a given trait. Suppose, for example, that we want to know if markets populated with individuals prone to preference reversals are more erratic. The most effective way to find out will be to measure preference reversals in a within-subject design, merge the subjects into groups based on their responses, and then compare the behaviour of high-reversal groups to that of low-reversal groups.

2.5.1 Disadvantages of Within-Subject Designs

Naturally, within-subject designs have pitfalls as well as advantages. The negative aspects are generally associated with the fact that the individual, when facing the second treatment, may not be exactly identical to the individual who was exposed to the first treatment, precisely because the first treatment has changed the subject's mindset. Unlike in *Men in Black*, experimenters do not have a 'neuralyzer' that would allow them to un-ask a question in order to reset the individual to the initial state. Thus, a spillover effect might take place, the exposure to the first treatment and the response provided therein confounding the effect of the second treatment. This could happen in a number of ways. Firstly, it could be that one treatment represents a frame of reference for the second treatment. In particular, the subjects may realise that the two treatments are analogous in some way and so, from the normative viewpoint, their answers should be identical. This is clearly a risk in the bakery-versus-airport-sandwich experiment. While subjects could have been naturally inclined to provide a high WTP in the airport scenario and a low WTP in the bakery scenario, when asked both questions one by one, they may recognise that such a pattern of choices is poorly justified. They may thus want to raise the bakery WTP when it follows elicitation of the airport WTP or to lower the airport WTP when it follows the elicitation of the bakery WTP.

For a related example, suppose we investigate the effect of time pressure on decision-making under risk by asking the subject to make the same choice, first under a lax time limit, then, immediately, under a strict time limit. The subject is likely to remember what they thought or calculated and how they chose in the first case, rendering ineffective the time limit manipulation in the second trial.

Secondly, by contrast, the subjects may be affected by the so-called *experimenter demand effect*: they may suspect that the experimenter expects them to behave in a certain way and may be willing to, consciously or otherwise, follow these expectations. In the sandwich example, some subjects might suspect that the experimenter is trying to prove that the WTPs is higher in the airport scenario. This effect may be particularly strong when the questions are hypothetical, so that it does not cost anything to deliver what the subject believes the experimenter wants. While demand effects may also show up in between-subject design, they tend to be stronger in within-subject designs, because the subject gets to know more than one treatment, which makes it much easier to guess what the hypothesis is and act 'appropriately'. A typical situation is that demand effects artificially inflate differences between treatments. Indeed, the subject may think that the experimenter would not have cared to compare two treatments if the experimenter had not hoped for a treatment effect.

The motivation to behave consistently and the motivation to be a 'good subject' tend to contradict each other; the first dampens the treatment effect while the second exacerbates it. One could hope they may cancel each other out, but there is no good scientific reason to justify the hope that their pull in opposite directions is equal. Obviously, there is no guarantee for that nor is it easy to estimate these two effects. Moreover, even if they were to roughly balance each other out on aggregate, they may affect different individuals in very different ways, hence the individual treatment effect would be overestimated for some subjects and underestimated for other subjects.

Finally, there may be situations is which providing a frame of reference would *also* inflate the treatment effect, thus adding to the demand effect rather than contracting it. One well-known example is scope insensitivity. If different groups of respondents are asked how much they were willing to pay to save 2,000, or 20,000, or 200,000 migrating birds, the responses may be very similar, reflecting mostly their budget and a general attitude towards environmental protection, rather than the scope of the problem at hand, which is difficult to grasp without a frame of reference. However, in a within-subject design, the subjects would understand that saving 20,000 is ten times as beneficial as saving just 2,000, and so also substantially more valuable. In cases like that, debates about whether an effect is 'real' (given that it shows to a much greater extent in a between-subject design than the within-subject design) will probably never be brought to an end.

To the extent that spillovers are unwanted, the chief strategy to reduce them would be to make it harder for the subjects to link the two treatments. Some of the strategies involve introducing unrelated filler questions and small perturbations in the underlying values. For example, in the case of a choice between two lotteries with positive outcomes, adding one euro to all of them is very unlikely to reverse the preference, but it is likely to make it harder for the subjects to recall they have already made a choice in this situation. If we want the subject to independently make such a choice twice (in two different treatments), such a slight perturbation may be a good idea.

Some insight into the strength of spillovers may be gained by comparing responses across different orderings of treatments. If the behaviour is the same in a given treatment, no matter whether it is preceded by another treatment or not, the spillovers are probably limited. If there are differences in one treatment only, we may infer it is likely to be influenced by the other, but not the other way around. In the time pressure example, eliciting preference under a strict time limit, then under a lax time limit, is likely to help avoid confounds. This is the essence of the double response methods (Agranov et al. 2015; Krawczyk and Sylwestrzak 2018).

To the extent, though, that the time effect per se can affect behaviour (e.g. because subjects become more tired and bored), being forced to stick to one order of treatments may not be ideal. Moreover, if there are *more* than two scenarios and there is no single obvious 'order' variable to test for correlations, identifying the pattern of confounding may be tricky. Finally, there could be a different effect than that on the central tendency. In particular, the behaviour in subsequent trials may be less noisy because subjects learn to avoid mistakes over time. Then again, when the experiment gets too long, tiredness and boredom may trigger more erratic behaviour (which strongly suggests that a between-subject design should be considered instead).

Finally, yet another case in which within-subject design may be problematic is when the experiment pertains to a decision that in 'real life' an individual is likely to face only once. A between-subject experiment may have greater external validity then.

2.5.2 Can We Have Both?

This short overview seems to suggest there are more good reasons to use within-subject designs, but the optimal design choice depends very much on the problem at hand and the available resources. Running a within-subject experiment with a sample size that would have been sufficiently large for a between-subject experiment may be the safest choice, as it allows both within-subject comparisons and uncontaminated between-subject comparisons (i.e. those pertaining only to the first treatment a given subject faced).

3 Optimal Designs

Experimenters often benefit from formal criteria of optimality helping them choose from a plethora of available options. For example, with discrete choice experiments (DCEs), to be discussed in detail in the next section, there are usually far too many possible questions for the experimenter to expect a subject to be able to answer all of them; a set of questions which is, in some sense, optimal is chosen. This section discusses the standard criteria, those which have become known as *alphabet optimality* and Lindley's approach of Shannon information gain (SIG) (Lindley 1956). For alphabet optimality, since Bayesian analysis lends itself to data analysis for choice experiments (e.g. the random parameters model (RPM)), we discuss both classical alphabet optimality criteria and their Bayesian counterparts. Importantly, we show that the criteria require a full description of the model; if optimality is based on the assumption that a reduced model is true, then the optimal design will not allow for model checking and will not be reliable if the reduced model turns out to be inappropriate. We show this by considering optimal designs for simple linear regression. We then show how different optimality criteria lead to different designs for a one-way model where different treatments may incur different costs. Finally, we consider a very important criterion for optimal design, based on SIG, which was introduced to Bayesian experimental design by D. V. Lindley, where he shows that, under the SIG criterion, for an experiment in several sequential parts, the expected information from the whole experiment is the sum of the expected information gains from each part. This is the basic workhorse of Section 5, where we consider adaptive designs; the next question in the sequence is chosen, based on the answers already given, to maximise expected information.

3.1 Introduction

We aim to find a design X from the space of possible designs $\mathcal{X}$, which minimises some functional $\mathcal{F}$, namely the optimal design is $\operatorname{argmin}_{X \in \mathcal{X}} \mathcal{F}(X)$. The choice of $\mathcal{F}$ depends on the sense in which the design is optimal; which criterion do we choose for optimality? It also depends on the computational power available to solve the minimisation problem.

In straightforward settings (e.g. the classical standard factorial designs – one way model, Latin square, 2^k factorial, and fractional factorial designs), there are well-motivated standard designs available where the motivation is intuitive and the designs facilitate parameter estimation and hence prediction; they represent good 'all-around' designs, although they may not be optimal with respect to any particular criterion that an experimenter has in mind. When the situation becomes more involved, these designs may not be feasible.

In Section 4, we discuss DCEs, where it is not possible to consider all treatment combinations. For example, suppose we are interested in estimating how choice is affected by six factors (or attributes), each coming at three different levels. There are $3^6 = 729$ possible treatment combinations. Suppose we observe *binary* choices between these; there are $\frac{1}{2} \times 729 \times 728 = 265{,}356$ different pairs. Few respondents will be willing to sit long enough to answer 265,356 questions. Moreoever, many of these comparisons will be 'no-brainers' (or, more formally, cases of weak dominance). If we know that Option A is better than Option B on some attributes and not any different (taking the same levels) on remaining attributes, then asking a respondent to choose from them is mostly interesting as a way to check if they are still awake after so many choices.

Only a very small fraction of possible choice sets is thus presented and the question, of course, is which they should be. A natural idea is to randomise levels independently. This approach guarantees (with sufficient data) that we can identify the impact of each attribute, but it is not necessarily an optimal approach. In particular, it does not exclude comparisons involving dominance, from which we do not learn much. How do we measure how much we expect to learn?

When designing an experiment, we have to make several decisions before we collect data. These decisions are: which covariates are to be included in the model (and hence the number of unknown parameters) and the values of those covariates over which the experimenter has control. The key elements of the statistical model are as follows:

- A *response* variable Y (or vector $\boldsymbol{Y}$).
- A design of covariates X that the experimenter chooses.
- A parameter θ (or parameter vector $\boldsymbol{\theta}$) of interest. We split $\boldsymbol{\theta}$ into two parts, $\boldsymbol{\theta} = (\boldsymbol{\beta}, \boldsymbol{\sigma})$ where $\boldsymbol{\beta}$ denotes the model parameters (how the covariates influence the outcome) and $\boldsymbol{\sigma}$ the 'noise' (or dispersion) parameters. In a standard Gaussian model, $\boldsymbol{\sigma} = \sigma$, a single parameter, which is the standard deviation of the error. We choose the length of $\boldsymbol{\beta}$ when we decide on the model, but the parameters themselves are unknown and the aim of the design problem is to choose an experiment which gives as much information as possible about them.

Note: the matrix X may contain columns where the values are not chosen by the experimenter. For example, consider the Gaussian linear model $\boldsymbol{Y} = X\boldsymbol{\beta} + \boldsymbol{\epsilon}$ where $\boldsymbol{Y}$ is an n-vector of observations, $\boldsymbol{\epsilon} \sim N(0, \sigma^2 I_n)$. Suppose there is an *intercept* parameter β_0, so that

$$Y_i = \beta_0 + \sum_{j=1}^{p} x_{ij}\beta_j + \epsilon_i.$$

There are p covariates; the value of covariate j for run i is x_{ij}. The design matrix may be written as $X = (\mathbf{1}_n | \widetilde{X})$ where $\mathbf{1}_n$ denotes an n-vector with each element 1 and $\widetilde{X}$ is the $n \times p$ design matrix with entries $\widetilde{X}_{ij} = x_{ij}$. The mean value space $\mathcal{M} = \{X\boldsymbol{\beta} : \boldsymbol{\beta} \in \mathbb{R}^{p+1}\}$ is a $p+1$ dimensional subspace of $\mathbb{R}^n$ and the parameter vector $\boldsymbol{\beta}$ (which includes the intercept β_0) is a $p+1$ vector.

The experiment is designed to provide: (a) an estimator $\widehat{\boldsymbol{\theta}} = f(y, X)$ of $\boldsymbol{\theta}$, which is a function of the response and covariates and (b) the distribution of the estimator, which we denote by $\pi(\boldsymbol{\theta}|y, X)$. In the classical setting, $\widehat{\boldsymbol{\theta}}$ may be (for example) an ordinary least squares (OLS) estimator or maximum likelihood estimator, while in the Bayesian setting, $\pi(\boldsymbol{\theta}|y, X)$ is the posterior distribution and we use $\widehat{\boldsymbol{\theta}}$ to denote a random vector with this distribution. With prior $\pi(\boldsymbol{\theta})$ and data likelihood $p(\boldsymbol{y}|X,\boldsymbol{\theta})$ (the probability density for outcome $\boldsymbol{y}$, when an experiment with design X is carried out and $\boldsymbol{\theta}$ is the true parameter vector), the posterior distribution (by Bayes rule) is:

$$\pi(\boldsymbol{\theta}|\boldsymbol{y},X) = \frac{\pi(\boldsymbol{\theta})p(\boldsymbol{y}|\boldsymbol{\theta},X)}{\int \pi(\boldsymbol{\theta})p(\boldsymbol{y}|\boldsymbol{\theta},X)d\boldsymbol{\theta}}.$$

For experimental design, the decision comes in two parts; before data is collected, a design (say X) is chosen from a set of possible designs, say $\mathcal{X}$. An experiment is then run according to the design and data $\boldsymbol{y}$ is collected, where $\boldsymbol{y} \in \mathcal{Y}$; $\mathcal{Y}$ denotes the sample space. Based on the data, a conclusion d is reached, from a space $\mathcal{D}$ of possible conclusions (e.g. from p possible treatments, a decision as to whether one of them is significantly better than the others and, if so, which is best).

In the classical setting, optimality is framed in terms of loss functions and risk. Let be the data and $l(\boldsymbol{\theta},f(\boldsymbol{y},X);X)$ the *loss* incurred by making a decision $f(\boldsymbol{y};X)$ when the true parameter vector is $\boldsymbol{\theta}$, using design X; the design X and estimator $f(\boldsymbol{Y};X)$ chosen to minimise the risk; the true parameter value $\boldsymbol{\theta}$ is, a priori, unknown, where the *risk* for f is defined as:

$$R(\boldsymbol{\theta},f;X) = \mathbb{E}_{\boldsymbol{\theta}}[l(\boldsymbol{\theta},f(\boldsymbol{Y};X);X)]. \tag{3.1}$$

When parameters $\boldsymbol{\beta}$ are in view, a standard choice for $f(\boldsymbol{Y};X)$ would be the *maximum likelihood* estimator $\widehat{\boldsymbol{\beta}}_{ML}$ and, for the loss, $l(\boldsymbol{\theta},f(\boldsymbol{Y};X);X) = |\boldsymbol{\beta} - \widehat{\boldsymbol{\beta}}_{ML}|^2$ (squared error loss). Then:

$$R(\boldsymbol{\theta},f;X) = \mathbb{E}_{(\boldsymbol{\beta},\sigma^2)}[|\widehat{\boldsymbol{\beta}}_{ML} - \boldsymbol{\beta}|^2].$$

Formulating it as a Bayesian decision problem, we construct a *utility function* $u(\boldsymbol{\theta},X,\boldsymbol{y})$, representing the utility when data $\boldsymbol{y}$ is obtained, $\boldsymbol{\theta}$ is the parameter vector, and X is the design chosen. For a design X, the expected utility is given by:

$$U(X) = \int_{\mathcal{Y}}\int_{\Theta} u(\boldsymbol{\theta},X,\boldsymbol{y})p(\boldsymbol{y}|\boldsymbol{\theta},X)\pi(\boldsymbol{\theta})d\boldsymbol{\theta}d\boldsymbol{y}, \tag{3.2}$$

and the optimal design is $X^* = \operatorname{argmax}_X U(X)$ (the design that maximises $U(X)$). Here $p(\boldsymbol{y}|\boldsymbol{\theta},X)$ is the density for $\boldsymbol{y}$ given $\boldsymbol{\theta}$ and X and $\pi(\boldsymbol{\theta})$ is the prior density for $\boldsymbol{\theta}$.

We discuss various optimality criteria, so-called 'alphabet'-optimality (both classical and Bayesian) and also the SIG criterion introduced by Lindley (1956) for optimal design. The SIG criterion is of particular importance in the discussion of *adaptive designs* (Section 5), since it is based on consistency between splitting an experiment into several components and treating the experiment as a whole.

In general, we aim to estimate quantities which are functions of model parameters $\boldsymbol{\beta}$. For example, when studying WTP and labelling β_0 the coefficient of *price* and $\beta_1, \ldots, \beta_p$ the non-price attributes, we are interested in the quantity $\gamma_i := -\frac{\beta_i}{\beta_0}$, which measures the respondent's WTP *per unit cost* for non-price attribute i.

Having decided on X, we gather data $\boldsymbol{y} = (y_1, \ldots, y_n)'$. The Bayesian optimal design is the design which maximises the expected utility (3.2). Parameter estimation is an important objective. It is also a key step on the way to computing a *predictive distribution*, which predicts, with as much certainty as possible, where future observations lie.

In optimal design theory, the optimality (or design) criteria are often direct functions of the information matrix, chosen to optimise accuracy either for parameter estimates or prediction. Except for the simplest cases (e.g. Gaussian), the information matrix depends on the unknown parameters to be estimated. The Bayesian approach deals with this by placing a prior distribution over the parameters. In general, *Bayesian* optimal designs outperform *locally* optimal designs based on a single prior choice of parameter. It is intuitively clear why this should be the case, but the enhanced performance comes at substantial additional computational cost for calculating the design.

The algorithms for finding (at least approximately) an optimal design according to the criteria discussed in what follows and their implementation may be found in the **acebayes** package for R; see Overstall and Woods (2017) for a comprehensive treatment of the derivation of the algorithms and their use.

3.2 Alphabet Optimality

Some of the most popular critera are the so-called alphabet-optimality criteria. They can broadly be divided into two categories, those based on parameter estimation and those based on the *predictive distribution.*

Alphabet-optimality critera arose with the Gaussian linear model $\boldsymbol{Y} = X\boldsymbol{\beta} + \boldsymbol{\epsilon}$ in view, where $\boldsymbol{\epsilon} \sim N(0, \sigma^2 I_n)$, with respect to the performance of the OLS estimator $\widehat{\boldsymbol{\beta}}_{\text{OLS}} = (X'X)^{-1}X'\boldsymbol{Y} \sim N(\boldsymbol{\beta}, \sigma^2(X'X)^{-1})$. For this situation, the estimator $\widehat{\boldsymbol{\beta}}_{\text{OLS}}$ is unbiased and BLUE (best linear unbiased estimator) in the sense that, among unbiased estimators, this is the estimator that minimises $\text{Var}(\sum c_j \widehat{\beta_j})$ for any linear combination $\sum_j c_j \beta_j$ of the parameters. One important feature here is that $\text{Cov}(\widehat{\boldsymbol{\beta}}_{\text{OLS}}) = \sigma^2(X'X)^{-1}$ does not depend on $\boldsymbol{\beta}$ (the true value of the parameter) and the 'optimal' design will not depend on σ^2. Discrete choice experiments (where each response is a choice of a particular option from two or more) do not fall into this framework.

Criteria Based on Parameter Estimation

- **D-optimality** The most popular optimality criterion to design choice experiments is the D-optimality criterion. The D-optimality criterion seeks to maximise the *determinant* of the information matrix (equivalently, it minimises the determinant of the inverse).

  For the Gaussian linear model $\boldsymbol{Y} = X\boldsymbol{\beta} + \boldsymbol{\epsilon}$, $\boldsymbol{\epsilon} \sim N(\mathbf{0}, \sigma^2 I_n)$, we have

$$p(\boldsymbol{y}|\boldsymbol{\beta}, \sigma^2, X) = \frac{1}{(2\pi)^{n/2}\sigma^n} \exp\left\{-\frac{1}{2\sigma^2}(\boldsymbol{Y} - X\boldsymbol{\beta})'(\boldsymbol{Y} - X\boldsymbol{\beta})\right\},$$

  so that:

$$I(\boldsymbol{\beta}) = -\nabla_{\boldsymbol{\beta}}\nabla_{\boldsymbol{\beta}} \log p(y|\boldsymbol{\beta}, \sigma^2, X) = \frac{1}{\sigma^2}(X'X).$$

  A D-optimal design therefore maximises $\det(I(\boldsymbol{\beta}))$; equivalently, it minimises $\det((X'X)^{-1})$. Since $\text{Cov}(\widehat{\boldsymbol{\beta}}_{\text{OLS}}) = \sigma^2(X'X)^{-1}$, this is equivalent to finding the design which minimises $\det(\text{Cov}(\widehat{\boldsymbol{\beta}}_{\text{OLS}}))$.

  Let us turn to the Bayesian setting, with prior $\pi(\boldsymbol{\beta}, \sigma^2) = \pi_1(\boldsymbol{\beta}|\sigma^2)\pi_2(\sigma^2)$, where $\pi_1 \sim N(\boldsymbol{\beta}_0, \sigma^2\Omega_0^{-1})$ (using $\boldsymbol{\beta}_0$ to denote the prior mean). Usually $\pi_2 \sim$ Scale-Inv$\chi^2(\nu, \tau^2)$ (the scale inverse chi squared is the standard conjugate prior for an unknown variance), although the choice of π_2 does not affect the design and can therefore be safely omitted from the discussion. We let

$$J(\boldsymbol{\beta}) := -\nabla_{\boldsymbol{\beta}}\nabla_{\boldsymbol{\beta}} \log \pi(\boldsymbol{\beta}, \sigma^2) = \frac{1}{\sigma^2}(\Omega_0 + (X'X)),$$

  where $\nabla_{\boldsymbol{\beta}}\nabla_{\boldsymbol{\beta}}$ denotes taking the matrix of second derivatives. This is the Bayesian counterpart of the Fisher information matrix for the parameter vector $\boldsymbol{\beta}$ (the prior has been incorporated). We consider a utility function $u(\boldsymbol{\theta}, X) := \det(J(\boldsymbol{\beta}))$ and take a design that minimises $U(X)$ (defined by (3.2)). The Bayesian D-optimal design defined in this way maximises $\det(\Omega_0 + (X'X))$ (or, equivalently, minimises $\det((\Omega_0 + (X'X))^{-1})$.

  More generally, in the framework of maximising expected utility (3.2), we take the utility function for design X as the determinant of the Fisher information for the parameters of interest:

$$u(\boldsymbol{\theta}, X) = -\det\left(\mathbb{E}_{\boldsymbol{\theta}}\left[\nabla_{\boldsymbol{\beta}}\nabla_{\boldsymbol{\beta}} \log \pi(\boldsymbol{\theta}|X, \boldsymbol{Y})\right]\right). \tag{3.3}$$

  where the expectation $\mathbb{E}_{\boldsymbol{\theta}}$ is with respect to $p(\boldsymbol{y}|\boldsymbol{\theta}, X)$ (the utility therefore does not depend on $\boldsymbol{y}$).

For example, consider the *logistic regression* model.

Logistic Models Logistic models fall under the umbrella of *generalised linear models* and we refer to Agresti (2012) for a good treatment of this subject. The *logistic* model, in its simplest case, is a model for binary data, where $Y \sim \text{Be}(\pi)$ (Bernoulli trial) and the *success* probability π depends on covariates $\boldsymbol{x} = (x_1, \ldots, x_p) \in \mathbb{R}^p$. The model is said to be *logistic* if the *logit* function of the success probability for covariate values $\boldsymbol{x} = (x_1, \ldots, x_p)$ may be written as

$$\log \frac{\pi(\boldsymbol{x})}{1 - \pi(\boldsymbol{x})} = \sum_{j=1}^{p} x_j \beta_j \tag{3.4}$$

for a parameter vector $\boldsymbol{\beta} = (\beta_1, \ldots, \beta_p)'$. This is the model referred to where the utility (3.5) is suggested for a Bayesian D-optimal design. Other standard models for binary data are generated by taking $\pi(\boldsymbol{x}) = \Phi(\sum_j x_j \beta_j)$ where Φ is the cumulative distribution function (CDF) of a random variable. Two important examples generated in this way are:

- The *probit* model, where $\Phi(z) = \int_{-\infty}^{z} \frac{1}{\sqrt{2\pi}} \exp\left\{-\frac{y^2}{2}\right\} dy$ (the standard normal CDF) and
- The *Gumbel* or *extreme value* model, where $\Phi(z) = \exp\{-\exp\{z\}\}$, so that

$$\log\left(-\log \pi\left(\sum_j x_j \beta_j\right)\right) = \sum_j x_j \beta_j.$$

The optimal design depends strongly on the model specification; a design that is optimal for model (3.4) will not necessarily be optimal for a probit or extreme value model.

For the logistic regression model, we have $Y_1, \ldots, Y_n$ independent Bernoulli trias, where $Y_i \sim \text{Be}(\pi(\boldsymbol{x}_i))$, $\boldsymbol{x}_i = (x_{i1}, \ldots, x_{ip})'$ denotes the covariate values for Y_i. We therefore have:

$$p(\boldsymbol{y}|\boldsymbol{\beta}, X) = \exp\left\{\sum_{i=1}^{n} \sum_{j=1}^{p} y_i x_{ij} \beta_j + \sum_{i=1}^{n} \log(1 - \pi_i(x_{i.}))\right\}.$$

A standard choice of prior is to take independence of the parameters under the prior and $\beta_j \sim N(\beta_{j,0}, s_j^2)$ for $j = 1, \ldots, p$. and (3.3) becomes:

$$u(\boldsymbol{\beta}, X) = \det\left(X' W(\boldsymbol{\beta}) X + \text{Diag}\left(\frac{1}{s_1^2}, \ldots, \frac{1}{s_p^2}\right)\right), \tag{3.5}$$

where $W(\boldsymbol{\beta}) = \text{Diag}(\pi_1(1-\pi_1), \ldots, \pi_n(1-\pi_n))$. The first part is from the Fisher information and the second part is from the prior. The important point to note is that for logistic regression, unlike the Gaussian case, the Fisher information depends on $\boldsymbol{\beta}$. With prior $\pi(\boldsymbol{\beta})$, the utility to be maximised is $U(X)$ from (3.2).

For optimal estimates of a vector $\boldsymbol{\gamma}(\boldsymbol{\theta})$ of length p, the *Bayesian* D-criterion value, known as the D_B- criterion value, is:

$$D_B = \int_{\Theta} \left(\det\left(I^{-1}(X, \boldsymbol{\gamma}(\boldsymbol{\theta}))\right)\right)^{1/p} \pi(\boldsymbol{\theta}) d\boldsymbol{\theta}, \tag{3.6}$$

where the exponent $1/p$ is inserted to ensure that the value is independent of the dimension p of the vector $\boldsymbol{\gamma}$. Minimising this value results in the D_B-optimal design.

D_s optimality is a variant of D-optimality, where we base the utility on a relevant *subset* of the parameters and minimise the determinant of the covariance matrix of this subset.

- **A-optimality**

An A-optimal design (classical setting) is a design which minimises the trace of the inverse of the information matrix. (For the Gaussian linear model, an A-optimal design is one which minimises $\text{Trace}((X'X)^{-1})$, which is equivalent to the design which minimises $\text{Tr}(\text{Cov}(\widehat{\boldsymbol{\beta}}))$, where $\widehat{\boldsymbol{\beta}} = (X'X)^{-1}X'\boldsymbol{Y}$ is BLUE).

For Bayesian A-optimality (general setting), let $\boldsymbol{\beta}_{\text{MEP}} = \int \boldsymbol{\beta}\pi(\boldsymbol{\theta}|\boldsymbol{y}, X) d\boldsymbol{\theta}$ denote the *mean posterior estimate* of $\boldsymbol{\beta}$); then a Bayesian A-optimal design is a design which minimises $U(X)$ of (3.2) with the *negative squared error loss* utility function:

$$u_{\text{NSEL}}(\boldsymbol{\beta}, X) = -(\boldsymbol{\beta} - \boldsymbol{\beta}_{\text{MEP}})'(\boldsymbol{\beta} - \boldsymbol{\beta}_{\text{MEP}}). \tag{3.7}$$

Note that, for the Gaussian linear model with prior $\pi(\boldsymbol{\beta}, \sigma^2) = \pi_1(\boldsymbol{\beta}|\sigma^2)\pi_2(\sigma^2)$, $\pi_1(\boldsymbol{\beta}|\sigma^2) \sim N(\boldsymbol{\beta}_0, \sigma^2\Omega_0^{-1})$ ($\boldsymbol{\beta}_0$ denotes prior mean) and $\pi_2(\sigma^2)$ is the prior over the variance parameter σ^2, we have

$$\boldsymbol{\beta}_{\text{MEP}} = \int \boldsymbol{\beta}\pi_1(\boldsymbol{\beta}|\sigma^2) d\boldsymbol{\beta};$$

$\boldsymbol{\beta}_{\text{MEP}}$ does not depend on $\boldsymbol{\sigma}$. the design is A-optimal if and only if it minimises $\text{Trace}((\Omega_0 + (X'X))^{-1})$ (irrespective of the prior π_2 over σ^2); this is equivalent to minimising the utility:

$$U_{\text{Gauss}}(X) = -\int_{\mathcal{Y}} \int_{\Theta} (\boldsymbol{\beta} - \boldsymbol{\beta}_{\text{MEP}})'(\boldsymbol{\beta} - \boldsymbol{\beta}_{\text{MEP}}) p(\boldsymbol{y}|\boldsymbol{\theta}, X) \pi_1(\boldsymbol{\beta}|\sigma^2) d\boldsymbol{\beta} d\boldsymbol{y}. \tag{3.8}$$

Bayesian A-optimality clearly carries over easily to other settings (e.g. weighted least squares regression, generalised linear models); the negative squared error loss utility function u_{NSEL} is well defined and the expected utility $U(X)$ can be approximated using either deterministic numerical integration techniques or Monte Carlo methods.

- **Pseudo-Bayesian-A optimality** Following (3.2), a Bayesian A-optimal design for estimating a vector $\boldsymbol{\gamma}(\boldsymbol{\theta})$ whose components are functions of the model parameters $\boldsymbol{\theta}$, maximises:

$$U(X) = -\int_{\mathcal{Y}}\int_{\Theta}(\gamma - \mathbb{E}[\gamma|\mathbf{y}, X])'(\gamma - \mathbb{E}[\gamma|\mathbf{y}, X])p(\mathbf{y}|\boldsymbol{\theta}, X)\pi(\boldsymbol{\theta})d\boldsymbol{\theta}d\mathbf{y},$$

where the expectation is with respect to the posterior. In most situations that are different from the Gaussian setting where $\boldsymbol{\gamma} = \boldsymbol{\beta}$, this problem presents serious computational difficulties and hence the utility u_{NSEL} is replaced by a utility that does not depend on $\mathbf{y}$:

$$u_{\text{NSEL.A}}(\boldsymbol{\gamma}, \mathbf{y}, X) := -\text{tr}\left(\Gamma^{-1}(X, \boldsymbol{\gamma})\right).$$

A design that is optimal with this utility function is a *pseudo-Bayesian-A optimal* design. The A_B-optimal design minimises:

$$A_B = \int_{\Theta}\text{trace}(\Gamma^{-1}(X, \boldsymbol{\gamma})\pi(\boldsymbol{\theta})d\boldsymbol{\theta}. \tag{3.9}$$

- **C-optimality** In many situations, it is not the parameters in and of themselves that are of interest, but rather functions of the parameters (these functions may be linear or non-linear). As we pointed out, in WTP experiments, with a vector of parameters $\boldsymbol{\beta}$, β_0 is often the coefficient of price, while $\beta_1, \ldots, \beta_p$ represents non-price attributes. We may be interested in $\gamma = (\gamma_1, \ldots, \gamma_p)'$, where $\gamma_i = -\frac{\beta_i}{\beta_0}$, which measures the respondent's WTP *per unit cost* for non-price attribute *i*.

  A C-optimal design is a design that is optimal for *functions* of the parameters, namely a design that is optimal for $\boldsymbol{\gamma}$ rather than for $\boldsymbol{\beta}$. This could be D- or A-optimality for $\boldsymbol{\gamma}$, depending on preference.

- **E-optimality** In the classical setting, for the Gaussian model, E-optimality is defined as choosing the design which minimises the largest eigenvalue of $(X'X)^{-1}$, which corresponds to minimising the maximum eigenvalue of $\text{Cov}(\widehat{\boldsymbol{\beta}})$. Equivalently, we take the design which minimises

$$\max_{\mathbf{e}:\sum_i e_i^2=1} \text{Var}\left(\sum_i e_i\widehat{\beta}_i\right) = \mathbf{e}'\text{Cov}(\widehat{\boldsymbol{\beta}})\mathbf{e} = \sigma^2\mathbf{e}'(X'X)^{-1}\mathbf{e}. \tag{3.10}$$

The maximising $\mathbf{e}$ in (3.10) is the eigenvector of $\text{Cov}(\widehat{\boldsymbol{\beta}})$ corresponding to the largest eigenvalue.

More generally, to find an E-optimal design for a vector $\boldsymbol{\gamma}$ (where each component of the vector is a function of the parameters), find the design X which maximises the utility function:

$$u(\boldsymbol{\theta}, X) = \max_{\boldsymbol{e}: \|\boldsymbol{e}\|=1} \left(-\boldsymbol{e}' \left(\mathbb{E}_{\boldsymbol{\theta}} \left[\nabla_{\gamma} \nabla_{\gamma} \log \pi(\boldsymbol{\theta}|X, \boldsymbol{y})\right]\right) \boldsymbol{e}\right), \tag{3.11}$$

where $\|\boldsymbol{e}\|^2 = \sum_i e_i^2$. This $\boldsymbol{e}$ is an eigenvector corresponding to the largest eigenvalue. In the classical setting, a reference parameter value $\boldsymbol{\theta}$ is used (i.e. a particular parameter value chosen by the user). For Bayesian E-optimality, a prior π over $\boldsymbol{\theta}$ is incorporated in the usual way.

- **S-optimality** This criterion considers the mutual column orthogonality of X and the determinant of the information matrix.

Criteria Based on Predictive Distribution

- **G-optimality** The choice of X is *G-optimal* if it minimises the maximum value of the variance of the *predictive distribution* of $Y(\underline{x})$ where $\underline{x}$ is one of the rows of X.

  For example, for linear models $\boldsymbol{Y} = X\boldsymbol{\beta} + \boldsymbol{\epsilon}$ where $\boldsymbol{\epsilon} \sim N(0, \sigma^2 I_n)$, $\boldsymbol{\beta}$ a p-vector, X an $n \times p$ matrix of rank p, $n > p$, the MLE of $\boldsymbol{\beta}$ is $\widehat{\boldsymbol{\beta}} = (X'X)^{-1}X'\boldsymbol{Y}$, and the predicted values are $\widehat{\boldsymbol{Y}} = X(X'X)^{-1}X'\boldsymbol{Y}$; the predictive distribution is the distribution of $\widehat{\boldsymbol{Y}}$, which is

  $$N(X\boldsymbol{\beta}, \sigma^2 X(X'X)^{-1}X').$$

  The matrix $H := X(X'X)^{-1}X'$ is the projection matrix known as the *hat* matrix, so called because it puts the hat onto $\boldsymbol{Y}$. Hence $\widehat{\boldsymbol{Y}} = H\boldsymbol{Y} \sim N(X\boldsymbol{\beta}, \sigma^2 H)$ (note: H is idempotent: $H^2 = H$ and $H' = H$) and the G-optimal design is the design that minimises the largest value of the diagonal of H.

  In the Bayesian setting for this model, where we assume a prior $\pi(\boldsymbol{\beta}, \sigma^2) = \pi_1(\boldsymbol{\beta}|\sigma^2)\pi_2(\sigma^2)$ where $\pi_1(\boldsymbol{\beta}|\sigma^2) \sim N(\boldsymbol{\beta}_0, \sigma^2\Omega_0^{-1})$, the posterior covariance of $\boldsymbol{\beta}$ is $\sigma^2(\Omega_0 + (X'X))^{-1}$ and the G-optimality criterion is to locate the design which minimises $\sup_{c \in \text{suppt}(X), \sum c_i^2 = 1} c(\Omega_0^{-1} + (X'X))^{-1}c'$ where $c \in \text{suppt}(X)$ denotes that c is a linear combination of the rows of X.
- **I-optimality** Here we minimise prediction variance over the space of designs available.
- **V-optimality** Here we minimise prediction variance over a set of specific points.

We discuss G- and V-optimality at greater length in Section 4, with specific reference to designs of DCEs.

3.2.1 Example: Simple Linear Regression and Alphabet Optimality

In this Element, the emphasis is on optimal designs for choice experiments, which typically present the subject with two or three choices (alternative 1, alternative 2, often there is also the possibility to reject both the alternatives) which fall within the framework of generalised linear models. The Fisher information takes the form $X'W(\boldsymbol{\beta})X$, where $W(\boldsymbol{\beta})$ is a diagonal matrix of weights. To illustrate the strengths and weaknesses of these optimality criteria, the computations are simplified enormously if $W(\boldsymbol{\beta}) = I$ (i.e. the identity matrix) and where X is simply an $n \times 2$ matrix (n observations with two parameters). The general principles can therefore all be observed by considering the simple linear regression model fitting only two parameters (intercept and slope), where the optimality criteria are based on the 2×2 matrix $X'X$. This shows forth the general principle that, while optimal designs give optimality *provided the model is correct*, they give absolutely no possibility for model checking. For illustration, we therefore limit consideration to the simple linear regression model $\boldsymbol{Y} = X\boldsymbol{\beta} + \boldsymbol{\epsilon}$, where

$$X = \begin{pmatrix} 1 & x_1 \\ \vdots & \vdots \\ 1 & x_n \end{pmatrix}, \qquad \boldsymbol{\beta} = \begin{pmatrix} \beta_0 \\ \beta_1 \end{pmatrix} \qquad \boldsymbol{\epsilon} \sim N(0, \sigma^2 I_n),$$

and show properties of the optimal design for the various criteria. This is the model for a single covariate; a response $Y(x)$ when the covariate takes value x is modelled as $Y(x) = \beta_0 + \beta_1 x + \epsilon$ where the ϵ's are independent for different runs and $\epsilon \sim N(0, \sigma^2)$.

The basic message is that if the model is known, then designs that are optimal according to alphabet-optimality criteria will produce the sharpest estimators for the relevant parameters (according to the selected criteria), but the designs may be rather poor if the model itself is uncertain and may not lend themselves to diagnostics for checking the model.

For simple linear regression, $X'X = n \begin{pmatrix} 1 & \overline{x} \\ \overline{x} & \overline{x^2} \end{pmatrix}$ where $\overline{x} = \frac{1}{n}\sum_{j=1}^n x_j$ and $\overline{x^2} = \frac{1}{n}\sum_{j=1}^n x_j^2$. Using $\mathrm{Var}(x) = \overline{x^2} - \overline{x}^2$, we have: $(X'X)^{-1} = \frac{1}{n\mathrm{Var}(x)} \begin{pmatrix} \overline{x^2} & -\overline{x} \\ -\overline{x} & 1 \end{pmatrix}$ so that, for the classical setting,

$$\begin{pmatrix} \widehat{\beta}_0 \\ \widehat{\beta}_1 \end{pmatrix} \sim N\left(\begin{pmatrix} \beta_0 \\ \beta_1 \end{pmatrix}, \frac{\sigma^2}{n\mathrm{Var}(x)} \begin{pmatrix} \overline{x}^2 + \mathrm{Var}(x) & -\overline{x} \\ -\overline{x} & 1 \end{pmatrix} \right).$$

For the estimates of β_0, β_1 and their covariance, this gives:

$$\mathrm{Var}(\widehat{\beta}_0) = \sigma^2 \left(\frac{\overline{x^2}}{n\mathrm{Var}(x)} + \frac{1}{n} \right), \quad \mathrm{Var}(\widehat{\beta}_1) = \frac{\sigma^2}{n\mathrm{Var}(x)}, \quad \mathrm{Cov}(\widehat{\beta}_0, \widehat{\beta}_1) = -\frac{\sigma^2 \overline{x}}{n\mathrm{Var}(x)}.$$

We can see that Var(x) is important here; if all the values $x_1, \ldots, x_n$ are approximately equal to $\bar{x}$ (so that Var(x) is small), then the variances of the parameter estimators will be large.

For the Bayesian setting, we take a prior distribution $\pi(\boldsymbol{\beta}) \sim N(\boldsymbol{\beta}_0, \sigma^2\Omega_0^{-1})$ for a fixed 2×2 invertible matrix Ω_0 (with a prior over σ^2) which updates to:

$$\pi(\boldsymbol{\beta}|\boldsymbol{y}, X) \sim N\left((X'X + \Omega_0)^{-1})(\Omega_0\boldsymbol{\beta}_0 + X'\boldsymbol{y}), \sigma^2(X'X + \Omega_0)^{-1}\right).$$

Let $\Omega_0 = \begin{pmatrix} \omega_{00} & \omega_{01} \\ \omega_{01} & \omega_{11} \end{pmatrix}$ so that

$$X'X + \Omega_0 = \begin{pmatrix} n + \omega_{00} & n\bar{x} + \omega_{01} \\ n\bar{x} + \omega_{01} & n\overline{x^2} + \omega_{11} \end{pmatrix}.$$

Let $a = \frac{n\bar{x}+\omega_{01}}{n+\omega_{00}}$ and $b = \frac{n\overline{x^2}+\omega_{11}}{n+\omega_{00}}$ and $v = b - a^2$. Then

$$(X'X + \Omega_0)^{-1} = \frac{1}{(n + \omega_{00})v} \begin{pmatrix} a^2 + v & -a \\ -a & 1 \end{pmatrix}. \tag{3.12}$$

Note In this set-up, the prior can be considered as information from an independent 'virtual' sample of size ω_{00}, where the average of the covariate values is $\frac{\omega_{01}}{\omega_{00}}$ (corresponding to $\bar{x}$ for the virtual sample) and the variance of the covariate values is $\frac{\omega_{11}}{\omega_{00}} - \left(\frac{\omega_{01}}{\omega_{00}}\right)^2$ (corresponding to Var(x) for the virtual sample). The quantity a is therefore the *overall* average of all covariate values (virtual and actual sample), while v is the *overall* variance of all covariate values (virtual and actual sample).

Let us consider the various optimality criteria for this example, both for the classical setting and for the Bayesian setting described earlier in this Element.

- **D-optimality** For the classical setting,

$$\det(\mathrm{Cov}(\widehat{\boldsymbol{\beta}})) = \frac{\sigma^4}{n^2\mathrm{Var}(x)},$$

while, in the Bayesian setting (taking $\widehat{\boldsymbol{\beta}}$ as a random vector whose distribution is the posterior over $\boldsymbol{\beta}$) and using the notation defined in Equation (3.12),

$$\det(\mathrm{Cov}(\widehat{\boldsymbol{\beta}})) = \frac{\sigma^4}{(n + \omega_{00})^2 v}.$$

Here, D-optimality gives us something quite intuitive; we should find a design which maximises Var(x) in the classical setting and v in the Bayesian.

An Obvious Problem While D-optimality gives a design that is optimal *provided the model is correct*, it delivers a design that is useless for model *checking*. Indeed, suppose we have a covariate x which takes possible values in $\{1,\ldots,9\}$ and we have an even number of observations $n = 2m$. The optimal design here is clear: take m observations with covariate value $x = 1$ and m observations with covariate value 9. This is the design that maximises $\text{Var}(x)$ (and hence minimises the objective).

With such a design, where only two values of the covariate are considered (at the extreme ends, in order to maximise $\text{Var}(x)$), it is impossible to check whether the *linear* model $Y(x) = \beta_0 + \beta_1 x + \epsilon$ in fact holds; the D-optimal design only gives us information for values $x = 1$ and $x = 9$ and we are left without any information at all to apply the standard diagnostics for checking whether the straight line plus IID noise is actually a good model. If the true model were $Y = \beta_0 + \beta_1 x + \beta_2 x^2 + \epsilon$, we would have no way of checking this with the data from a D-optimal design for the model $Y = \beta_0 + \beta_1 x + \epsilon$.

If there is any doubt about whether a reduced model is suitable, the D-optimal design for the *full* model should be computed. In the experimental design setting, this means (for example) that if we want to test whether there are important interaction effects, they have to be included in the model when computing the D-optimal design.

- **A-optimality** The A-optimality criterion ignores possible covariance between the parameter estimates; in this case, an A-optimal design minimises the trace of the covariance. In the classical setting, this means minimising:

$$\frac{\text{Var}(x) + \overline{x}^2 + 1}{\text{Var}(x)} = 1 + \frac{\overline{x}^2 + 1}{\text{Var}(x)}.$$

Again, if the covariate values are chosen in an interval $[z_1, z_2]$, then the optimal design chooses a proportion α with covariate value z_1 and a proportion $1 - \alpha$ with covariate value z_2, so that $\overline{x} = \alpha z_1 + (1 - \alpha)z_2$. The solution is obtained by finding the α that minimises:

$$\frac{1 + (\alpha z_1 + (1 - \alpha)z_2)^2}{\alpha(1 - \alpha)(z_1 - z_2)^2}.$$

For model checking, an A-optimal design has the same problems as a D-optimal design; the design that minimises the objective does not permit diagnostics which check whether the model is correct.

- **C-optimality** We consider C-optimality in a straightforward linear setting, for linear functions of the parameters. We want to minimise $\text{Var}(c_0\widehat{\beta_0} + c_1\widehat{\beta_1})$ for a given (c_0, c_1). For example, suppose we are interested in precise estimates of the average value of future observations with covariate value z. Here $\mathbb{E}[Y(z)] = \beta_0 + \beta_1 z$, so that $(c_0, c_1) = (1, z)$. If the aim is to obtain sharp estimates on $\mathbb{E}[c_0\widehat{\beta}_0 + c_1\widehat{\beta}_1]$, then we choose $x_1, \ldots, x_n$ to minimise:

$$\begin{aligned}\mathrm{Var}(c_0\widehat{\beta}_0 + c_1\widehat{\beta}_1) &= \frac{\sigma^2}{n\mathrm{Var}(x)}\left(c_0^2\overline{x}^2 + c_0^2\mathrm{Var}(x) + c_1^2 - 2c_0c_1\overline{x}\right) \\ &= \frac{\sigma^2}{n}\left(c_0^2 + \frac{(c_0\overline{x} - c_1)^2}{\mathrm{Var}(x)}\right).\end{aligned}$$

Any design satisfying $c_0\overline{x} = c_1$ (e.g. choose $x_1 = \ldots = x_n = \frac{c_1}{c_0}$) minimises the objective. This is not a big surprise; if we want to estimate $\mathbb{E}[Y(z)] = \beta_0 + \beta_1 z$, so that $c_0 = 1$ and $c_1 = z$ (and we are not interested in any other covariate value), then the natural experiment would be n repetitions, where $x_1 = \ldots = x_n = z$.

Bayesian C-optimality, for a fixed $c = (c_0, c_1)$ requires the design $(x_1, \ldots, x_n)$ which minimises:

$$\frac{(c_0 a - c_1)^2}{v},$$

where $a = \frac{n\overline{x}+\omega_{01}}{n+\omega_{00}}$ and v are defined for Equation (3.12). Choosing any design such that $\overline{x} = \frac{\frac{c_1}{c_0}(n+\omega_{00})-\omega_{01}}{n}$ will satisfy C-optimality for a particular linear combination $c = (c_0, c_1)$.

- **E-optimality** Returning to Equations (3.10) and (3.12) (considering the Bayesian setting), an E-optimal design is a design which minimises:

$$\frac{1}{(n+\omega_{00})v}\max_{(e_0,e_1):e_0^2+e_1^2=1}(e_0, e_1)\begin{pmatrix} a^2+v & -a \\ -a & 1\end{pmatrix}\begin{pmatrix} e_0 \\ e_1\end{pmatrix}.$$

The maximising (e_0, e_1) is the eigenvector corresponding to the largest eigenvalue which (of course) depends on a and v. While D-optimality considers the determinant, which is the product of eigenvalues, and A-optimality considers the trace, which is the sum of eigenvalues, E-optimality reduces the problem by selecting a single eigenvalue, which is the largest eigenvalue.

The computation is omitted; the expression to be minimised then depends only on a and v, decreasing in v, which turns out (unsurprisingly) to have the same properties as D and A optimisation; if the values are restricted to an interval $x_i \in [l_-, l_+]$, the E-optimal design will choose extreme values to maximise Var(x) (Classical) or v (Bayesian, from (3.12)); a proportion α will satisfy $x_i = l_-$; and a proportion $1 - \alpha$ will satisfy $x_i = l_+$. As with other criteria, the E-optimal design therefore restricts itself to two values and does not give any possibility for model checking.

- **S-optimality** Column orthogonality means that we would like to choose our covariates $x_1,\ldots,x_n$ such that $\overline{x} = 0$ (i.e. $(\mathbf{1}_n, x) = 0$). For such designs, the whole business simplifies and:

$$(X'X)^{-1} = \frac{1}{n}\begin{pmatrix} 1 & 0 \\ 0 & \frac{1}{\overline{x^2}} \end{pmatrix}.$$

Column orthogonality gives: $\widehat{\beta}_0 \perp \widehat{\beta}_1$ (i.e. the estimators are independent). Also, with such column orthogonality, $\widehat{\beta}_0 = \overline{Y}$ (simply the sample average) and the only design consideration is, within the constraint $\overline{x} = 0$, to maximise $\overline{x^2}$ to get the optimal estimator of β_1.

Designs which have column orthogonality (orthogonal contrast designs such as 2^k experiments) are often easier to deal with.

We now illustrate the criteria which are based on the predictive distribution with this simple two-parameter example, noting that all the basic principles for a more general setting are already present in the two-parameter example.

- **G-optimality** Consider a new observation where the covariate is z; consider σ^2 fixed and known. $\boldsymbol{Y}$ is the n-vector of observations and X is the design matrix. Hence, we use $\pi(\boldsymbol{\beta}|X, \boldsymbol{Y})$ to denote the distribution of the estimator of $\boldsymbol{\beta}$. This is the distribution of $\widehat{\boldsymbol{\beta}}$, the maximum likelihood estimator, in the classical case and the posterior distribution in the Bayesian setting. The predictive distribution of $y(z)$ (new observation y with covariate value z, using $\boldsymbol{Y}$ to denote the n-vector of observations on which the parameter estimates are based) is:

$$p(y|z) = \frac{\int \pi(\boldsymbol{\beta}|\boldsymbol{Y}, X)p(y|\boldsymbol{\beta}, z)d\boldsymbol{\beta}}{\int\int \pi(\boldsymbol{\beta}|\boldsymbol{Y}, X)p(y|\boldsymbol{\beta}, z)d\boldsymbol{\beta}dy}.$$

In the classical setting, $\pi(\boldsymbol{\beta}|y, X) \sim N(\widehat{\boldsymbol{\beta}}, \sigma^2(X'X)^{-1})$. For covariate value z, a new observation y has distribution $p(y|\boldsymbol{\beta}, z) \sim N(\beta_0 + \beta_1 z, \sigma^2)$. The density of the predictive distribution is therefore:

$$p(y|X, \boldsymbol{Y}, z) \sim N\left(\widehat{\beta}_0 + \widehat{\beta}_1 z, \sigma^2\left(1 + \frac{1}{n} + \frac{(\overline{x} - z)^2}{n\mathrm{Var}(x)}\right)\right).$$

In the Bayesian setting, the predictive distribution is:

$$p(y|X, \boldsymbol{Y}, z) \sim N\left(\beta_{0,\mathrm{MEP}} + \beta_{1,\mathrm{MEP}} z, \sigma^2\left(1 + \frac{1}{n+k} + \frac{(A - z)^2}{(n+k)B}\right)\right),$$

where $\begin{pmatrix} \beta_{0,\mathrm{MEP}} \\ \beta_{1,\mathrm{MEP}} \end{pmatrix}$ is the mean of the posterior $\pi(\boldsymbol{\beta}|X, \boldsymbol{Y}, z)$. The G-optimality criterion is therefore the same as C-optimality, where $c = (1, z)$, and is therefore useless for producing a design that allows diagnostics to check whether the model is reasonable.

- **I- and V-optimality** These are the same as G-optimality, except that we have a reduced set of designs over which to make the optimisation.

3.2.2 Optimality with Constraints: One-Way Design

So far, we have considered the standard alphabet-optimality criteria. In practice, though, there are often budget constraints. Some treatments may be more expensive than others and we may be working with a limited budget.

Constrained optimisation is a substantially harder problem than the same optimisation problem without constraints. We restrict the discussion to the one-way means model:

$$Y_{ij} = \mu_i + \epsilon_{ij} \qquad j = 1, \ldots, n_i \qquad i = 1, \ldots, p,$$

where there are p different treatments, n_i the number of subjects receiving treatment i, the ϵ_{ij}'s are taken to be IID. $N(0, \sigma^2)$, the treatment mean for treatment i is μ_i. We would like to find the optimal design when there is a limited budget B and a single experiment applying treatment i costs c_i. Hence, if n_i subjects receive treatment i, we have the constraint $\sum_{i=1}^{p} c_i n_i \leq B$. We consider the classical A-optimal and D-optimal designs for $\boldsymbol{\mu} := (\mu_1, \ldots, \mu_p)'$ subject to the constraint. Here we have $\widehat{\mu}_i = \overline{Y}_{i.} \sim N(\mu_i, \frac{\sigma^2}{n_i})$. Since they are independent, we have $\mathrm{Cov}(\boldsymbol{\mu}) = \sigma^2 \mathrm{diag}(\frac{1}{n_1}, \ldots, \frac{1}{n_p})$ (the covariance matrix is a diagonal matrix) so that its determinant (the criterion for D-optimality) is $\sigma^{2p} \prod_{i=1}^{p} \frac{1}{n_i}$ and its trace (the criterion for A-optimality) is $\sigma^2 \sum_{i=1}^{p} \frac{1}{n_i}$.

The two optimisation problems are slightly different. For D-optimality, the optimisation problem is:

$$\begin{aligned} &\text{minimise} && \textstyle\prod_{i=1}^{p} \frac{1}{n_i} \\ &\text{subject to} && \textstyle\sum_{i=1}^{p} c_i n_i \leq B, \end{aligned}$$

while for A-optimality, the problem is:

$$\begin{aligned} &\text{minimise} && \textstyle\sum_{i=1}^{p} \frac{1}{n_i} \\ &\text{subject to} && \textstyle\sum_{i=1}^{p} c_i n_i \leq B. \end{aligned}$$

A natural approach for these problems would be the so-called Lagrange multiplier approach. For the D-optimality problem, minimising $\prod_{i=1}^{p} \frac{1}{n_i}$ is equivalent to minimising $\log \prod_{i=1}^{p} \frac{1}{n_i} = -\sum_{j=1}^{p} \log n_i$, so we consider the problem of minimising

$$-\sum_{i=1}^{p} \log n_i + \lambda \sum_{i=1}^{p} c_i n_i,$$

solving it as an unconstrained problem and then choosing λ so that the constraint is satisfied. In this case,

$$-\frac{1}{n_i} + \lambda c_i = 0 \Rightarrow n_i = \frac{1}{\lambda c_i}.$$

Then $B = \sum_{i=1}^{p} c_i n_i = \frac{p}{\lambda} \Rightarrow \lambda = \frac{p}{B}$ giving a constrained D-optimal design of:

$$n_i = \frac{B}{pc_i} \qquad i = 1, \ldots, p.$$

Of course, the n_i's computed in this way are probably not integers; appropriate rounding should be done.

Computation for the constrained A-optimal design is similar; minimise

$$\sum_{i=1}^{p} \frac{1}{n_i} + \lambda \sum_{i=1}^{p} c_i n_i$$

so that $-\frac{1}{n_i^2} + \lambda c_i = 0 \Rightarrow n_i = \frac{1}{\sqrt{\lambda c_i}}$. Then λ is chosen such that $B = \sum c_i n_i = \frac{1}{\sqrt{\lambda}} \sum_{i=1}^{p} \sqrt{c_i}$ giving $\lambda = \frac{1}{B^2} \left(\sum_{i=1}^{p} \sqrt{c_i} \right)^2$ and the constrained A-optimal design is:

$$n_i = \frac{B}{\left(\sum_{j=1}^{p} \sqrt{c_j} \right) \sqrt{c_i}} \qquad i = 1, \ldots, p$$

(making minor alterations, rounding up or down to ensure that each n_i is an integer).

In the particular set-up of the homoscedastic one-way model, the problem is relatively simple to formulate and to solve; the method of Lagrange multipliers for this problem is straightforward. In general, though, constrained optimisation is not an easy problem and it is difficult to find packages which deal with alphabet-optimality subject to constraints. This is an important topic and should be a direction for fruitful future study.

3.3 Optimisation Based on Shannon Entropy

Another very important utility function for Bayesian optimality is the so-called SIG utility, defined by:

$$u_{\text{SIG}}(\boldsymbol{\beta}, \boldsymbol{y}, X) = \log \pi(\boldsymbol{\beta} | X, \boldsymbol{y}) - \log \pi(\boldsymbol{\beta}), \tag{3.13}$$

where $\pi(\boldsymbol{\beta})$ denotes the prior distribution over the parameters $\boldsymbol{\beta}$ and $\pi(\boldsymbol{\beta}|X,\boldsymbol{y})$ is the posterior, based on observations $\boldsymbol{y}$ and design X. This is used in (3.2) to provide an expected utility $U(X)$. The quantity u_{SIG} is simply the *mutual information* between $\boldsymbol{\beta}$ and $\boldsymbol{y}$, which we denote $I(\boldsymbol{\beta},\boldsymbol{y})$. If $\boldsymbol{\beta}$ and $\boldsymbol{y}$ are independent, then $u_{\text{SIG}} = 0$. It can be established (by Jensen's inequality) that the mutual information is non-negative. Furthermore, mutual information satisfies $I(\boldsymbol{\beta},\boldsymbol{\beta}) \geq I(\boldsymbol{\beta},\boldsymbol{y})$ for any random vector $\boldsymbol{y}$ (a random variable contains as much information about itself as any other random variable can provide).

3.3.1 The Contribution of D. V. Lindley

The utility u_{SIG} was suggested as a criterion for experimental design by D. V. Lindley in his seminal article (Lindley 1956), where he took the work of Shannon (1948) as his starting point for establishing a definition of the information provided by an experiment and, from this, a utility function with a useful and natural additive property.

If an experiment $\mathcal{E}$ is carried out in two parts, say $\mathcal{E}_1$ for the first part, and then a further experiment $\mathcal{E}_2$, then, Lindley postulated, the information from the whole experiment, denoted $\mathcal{I}(\mathcal{E})$, should satisfy an additive property:

$$\mathcal{I}(\mathcal{E}) = \mathcal{I}(\mathcal{E}_1) + \int \mathcal{I}(\mathcal{E}_2^{(y)}|\mathcal{E}_1,y)p_{\mathcal{E}_1}(y)dy,$$

where y denotes the outcome of $\mathcal{E}_1$ and $\mathcal{E}_2^{(y)}$ denotes the second experiment carried out when the outcome of $\mathcal{E}_1$ is y. $p_{\mathcal{E}_1}$ denotes the distribution for outcomes of $\mathcal{E}_1$ and $\mathcal{I}(\mathcal{E}_2^{(y)}|\mathcal{E}_1,y)$ denotes the additional information obtained when experiment $\mathcal{E}_2^{(y)}$ is carried out after outcome y was obtained from $\mathcal{E}_1$. Building on Shannon's earlier work, Lindley showed that u_{SIG} was the only utility that satisfied this.

The approach, based on SIG is precisely that adopted by Chapman et al. (2018) in DOSE (dynamically optimised sequential experimentation), an important and developing technique that we discuss in detail in Section 5.

The information which the researcher has before carrying out an experiment is expressed as a *prior* probability distribution, which we denote by π_Θ over a parameter space, which we denote by Θ; the true parameter value $\boldsymbol{\theta} \in \Theta$ is unknown and the aim of the experiment is to improve our knowledge about $\boldsymbol{\theta}$.

Let $\mathcal{Y}$ denote the space of possible outcomes of an experiment, with generic element $y \in \mathcal{Y}$. We assume that if the 'state of the world' (i.e. the value of the parameter, or parameter vector $\boldsymbol{\theta}$) is known, then the outcome of the experiment will be a random variable Y with probability distribution $p_{Y|\Theta}(.|\boldsymbol{\theta}) : \mathcal{Y} \to \mathbb{R}_+$ (where, for each $\boldsymbol{\theta} \in \Theta$, $p_{Y|\Theta}(.|\boldsymbol{\theta})$ is a probability mass function if $\mathcal{Y}$ is finite or countably infinite, or a density if Y is a continuous random variable). The unit $p_{Y|\Theta}(.|\boldsymbol{\theta})$ is basic; if we know $\boldsymbol{\theta}$, then we know the probability distribution of Y, the outcome of the experiment.

The quantity π_Θ is the prior distribution, which represents our information about $\boldsymbol{\theta}$ before the experiment takes place. If our experiment gives outcome

y, we update the prior to a posterior distribution over the parameter space; the *marginal* distribution for the outcome of the experiment is:

$$p_Y(y) = \int \pi_\Theta(\boldsymbol{\theta}) p_{Y|\Theta}(y|\boldsymbol{\theta}) d\boldsymbol{\theta},$$

and, by Bayes' rule, the posterior distribution over Θ, given outcome y is:

$$\pi_{\Theta|Y}(\boldsymbol{\theta}|y) = \frac{\pi_\Theta(\boldsymbol{\theta}) p_{Y|\Theta}(y|\boldsymbol{\theta})}{p_Y(y)}.$$

In experimental economics, our aim is usually to 'gain knowledge about the world' (to quote Lindley), by which he means that the distribution over the parameter space represents knowledge about the world, or problem under investigation; our experiment should be such that, when we update prior to posterior, this gives the best improvement of our knowledge of $\boldsymbol{\theta}$, subject to the restrictions on the experiments that we can carry out.

3.3.2 Shannon Entropy and Information

We now follow Lindley to show how the negative of *Shannon entropy* gives a convincing approach to the amount of information we have about a parameter if we know the probability distribution and why, when assessing the amount of information gained, the *Kullback–Leibler* divergence is a useful quantity.

Definition 3.1 (Shannon entropy) *For a distribution with density π_Θ over a parameter space $\Theta \subseteq \mathbb{R}^n$, the negative of the* Shannon entropy *is defined as:*

$$\boldsymbol{H}(\pi_\Theta) := -\int_\Theta \pi_\Theta(\boldsymbol{\theta}) \log \pi_\Theta(\boldsymbol{\theta}) d\boldsymbol{\theta}.$$

We follow Lindley by taking the negative of this quantity, which we call the *information* in the distribution:

$$\mathcal{I}(\pi_\Theta) = -\boldsymbol{H}(\pi_\Theta) = \int_\Theta \pi_\Theta(\boldsymbol{\theta}) \log \pi_\Theta(\boldsymbol{\theta}) d\boldsymbol{\theta}.$$

The negative sign in Shannon's definition is due to the fact that he is considering the *opposite* of information; Shannon's entropy is a measure of *disorder*. Shannon (1948) gives reasons why this is a good measure and we follow Lindley's description of Shannon's motivational arguments.

To simplify the discussion, suppose Θ is finite (so that π_Θ is a probability mass function and

$$\mathcal{I}(\pi_\Theta) = \sum_{\boldsymbol{\theta} \in \Theta} \pi_\Theta(\boldsymbol{\theta}) \log \pi_\Theta(\boldsymbol{\theta}).$$

Now consider the additional information required before the value of $\boldsymbol{\theta}$ is known and suppose that this information is provided in two stages:

Stage 1 Let $\Theta_1 \subset \Theta$ be a non-empty, strict subset of Θ where $\sum_{\theta \in \Theta_1} \pi_\Theta(\theta) \neq 0$ or 1. Suppose the first stage of the experiment tells us whether $\theta \in \Theta_1$ or $\theta \in \Theta \backslash \Theta_1$. The prior distribution over $(\Theta_1, \Theta\backslash\Theta_1)$ is $(\Pi, 1-\Pi)$, where $\Pi = \sum_{\theta \in \Theta_1} \pi_\Theta(\theta)$. Let us denote the information from the first stage as I_1.

Stage 2 After this, we perform a second experiment, which tells us the precise value of θ. Let us denote the information provided by the second stage as: $I_{2,1}$ if $\theta \in \Theta_1$, or $I_{2,2}$ if $\theta \in \Theta\backslash\Theta_1$. The distributions over Θ_1 and $\Theta\backslash\Theta_1$ are $\frac{\pi_\Theta(\theta)}{\Pi}$ and $\frac{\pi_\Theta(\theta)}{1-\Pi}$ respectively.

We require an information measure such that the information provided in the first stage and that the average amount in the second stage add up to the total information – that is:

$$I = I_1 + \Pi I_2 + (1-\Pi) I_3.$$

Shannon proves that (apart from arbitrary multiplicative constant) $I = \sum_{\theta \in \Theta} \pi_\Theta(\theta) \log \pi_\Theta(\theta)$ is the *only* function satisfying this property (together with a mild continuity property).

We can see that I, thus defined, has this property:

$$\begin{aligned}
I_1 &= \Pi \log \Pi + (1-\Pi)\log(1-\Pi) \\
I_2 &= \textstyle\sum_{\theta\in\Theta_1} \frac{\pi_\Theta(\theta)}{\Pi} \log \frac{\pi_\Theta(\theta)}{\Pi} = \frac{1}{\Pi}\left(\sum_{\theta\in\Theta_1} \pi_\Theta(\theta)\log \pi_\Theta(\theta)\right) - \log \Pi \\
I_3 &= \textstyle\sum_{\theta\in\Theta\backslash\Theta_1} \frac{\pi_\Theta(\theta)}{1-\Pi} \log \frac{\pi_\Theta(\theta)}{1-\Pi} = \frac{1}{1-\Pi}\left(\sum_{\theta\in\Theta\backslash\Theta_1} \pi_\Theta(\theta)\log \pi_\Theta(\theta)\right) - \log(1-\Pi),
\end{aligned}$$

and the identity $I = I_1 + \Pi I_2 + (1-\Pi) I_3$ follows directly.

After the experiment has been performed, a result y observed and the distribution over Θ updated to $\pi_{\Theta|Y}(.|y)$, the information is:

$$\mathcal{I}(\pi_{\Theta|Y}(.|y)) = \int_\Theta \pi_{\Theta|Y}(\theta|y) \log \pi_{\Theta|Y}(\theta|y) d\theta,$$

and the information *gain* is:

$$\mathcal{K}(y) = \mathcal{I}(\pi_{\Theta|Y}(.|y)) - \mathcal{I}(\pi_\Theta).$$

We assume that, given a true parameter value θ, the outcome y of an experiment is governed by a probability distribution $p_{Y|\Theta}(.|\theta)$. The information difference depends on the observation y. If we are choosing between different experiments, then clearly we do not know the outcome before we carry out the experiment. We therefore average the information difference over all outcomes for an experiment to get a suitable measure. After some computation,

$$\int \mathcal{K}(y) p_Y(y) dy = \mathbb{D}_{KL}(\pi_{\Theta|Y} p_Y \| \pi_\Theta p_Y).$$

(Here $p_Y \pi_{\Theta|Y} = \pi_\Theta p_{Y|\Theta}$ is the joint distribution over parameter space / state space.)

This is the Kullback–Leibler divergence between the *joint* distribution $\pi_\Theta p_{Y|\Theta}$ over $\Theta \times \mathcal{Y}$ and the product distribution $\pi_\Theta p_Y$ over $\Theta \times \mathcal{Y}$ (if the parameter and observation were independent, the Kullback–Leibler divergence would be zero; the experiment would provide no information).

The Kullback–Leibler divergence has several important properties which indicate that it is useful for measuring the gain of information from an experiment. Firstly, if f and g are two probability distributions over a state space $\mathcal{X}$, then $\mathbb{D}_{KL}(f\|g) \geq 0$, where the inequality is strict if f and g differ on a set of positive f probability. This follows from Jensen's inequality. Another property is the *additive* property, which was Shannon's basic reason for introducing the entropy functional. Let $\mathcal{E}$ denote an experiment which takes place in two parts, $\mathcal{E} = (\mathcal{E}_1, \mathcal{E}_2)$, where $\mathcal{E}_2$ is performed after $\mathcal{E}_1$. Let $\mathcal{K}_\mathcal{E}$ denote the average information provided by the whole experiment, $\mathcal{K}_{\mathcal{E}_1}$ the average information provided by the first part, and $\mathcal{K}_{\mathcal{E}_2|\mathcal{E}_1}$ the average additional information provided by the second, then:

$$\mathcal{K}_\mathcal{E} = \mathcal{K}_{\mathcal{E}_1} + \mathcal{K}_{\mathcal{E}_2|\mathcal{E}_1},$$

which follows by an easy computation.

3.4 Aspects of Optimal Design for Discrete Choice Experiments

In choice experiments, there are usually a very large number of possible choices. The optimality critera may be applied to obtain optimal designs, where each question admits three answers (choose option A, choose option B, refuse both A and B). The theory requires that responses to questions are *independent*. Section 2 deals with issues about between- and within- subject sampling and these should nuance the criteria for choosing an optimal design for choice experiments. We draw attention to the following.

- There is an R package **acebayes**, which is discussed in Overstall and Woods (2017), who wrote the package. This creates optimal designs where all parameters of interest are included. The design does what it says on the tin and is optimal according to the criterion selected.
- Different optimality criteria can give different designs. For example, we presented the one-way model (Section 3.2.2), where the total *cost* (and not the number of subjects) was fixed and different treatments had different costs.
- Bayesian designs are to be recommended, since they incorporate expert prior probability assessment information over parameters; classical designs for generalised linear models tend to optimise for a *fixed* parameter value

chosen in advance in all but the simplest (i.e. Gaussian) cases. The Bayesian update from prior to posterior gives a *consistent* approach to parameter uncertainty provided that the probability model for data generation is correct; any ad hoc element is clearly seen in the choice of prior.

- D- and A-optimal designs (and their Bayesian counterparts) are based on the Fisher information matrix (or corresponding Bayesian quantity). A good probability model for data generation is therefore essential. If data generation is properly described by the model, the design will be optimal according to the optimality criterion. If the model is incorrectly specified, then there can be serious problems, as we saw in the discussion of optimality criteria for simple linear regression. *All* the designs placed all the observations at extreme points; the optimal designs left no room at all for model *checking*; they were optimal only if the model was correct.
- For within-subject questioning, a subject will have a *memory* of previous questions, hence the responses to successive questions may not satisfy the 'independence' assumption upon which optimality criteria are based; if the same subject is presented with the same question twice (which may happen when alphabet-optimal design criteria are employed), it is difficult to see how to 'reset' the subject between the two questions. The subject has a memory of the previous answer and therefore may well give exactly the same answer without additional thought. In other words, the *error* will carry over to subsequent questions.

  The **acebayes** package has a useful feature: a function `limits` whereby the user can ensure that a row of the design matrix is not repeated (in the case of DCEs, a particular question is presented exactly once).
- Questions such as whether it is better to increase the number of subjects or increase the number of questions per subject depend on two things. We need good probability models for data generation; we also need some understanding of the psychology of the subjects – how many questions can a subject reasonably handle? Similarly, questions such as whether it is better to have one choice between four options or to elicit the preferred option through several binary-option questions largely depends on how accurate the answers are expected to be when the subject is faced with a larger number of choices. The whole raison d'être behind much of the theory of DCEs is that subjects are unlikely to be able to process effectively the contents of a large set of possible choices; asking questions where only three options are available (alternative A, alternative B, neither) may lead to more informative answers.
- 'No-brainer' questions (where a bundle where each attribute is worse than the alternative being offered and is at a higher price than the alternative)

should be excluded (unless, of course, they are included simply as a diagnostic to check whether the subject is giving credible answers). A standard algorithm for producing an optimal design may not discern such a question, but this should be clear to the user, who can program the algorithm to avoid such questions. The function `limits` in **acebayes** can be used to do this.
- Optimal design theory is intended for the situation where there are far too many possibilities to run a standard orthogonal design. The overwhelming reason for generating optimal designs for DCEs is that the total number of possible questions is very large and the set-up does not lend itself to standard orthogonal designs.

As we have seen, the entire theory of optimal design is based on the assumption of independent observations. This may be inappropriate for within-subject experiments (where errors are not necessarily independent). Substantial advances for DCEs could be made by considering *correlation* between errors for within-subject experiments and incorporating this into computation of the Fisher information. Another possibility is to define a distance between rows of the design matrix X and to find optimal designs *under constraints*, the constraints being that the rows of X are separated from each other by a suitable distance, so that responses can be seen as independent observations.

4 Discrete Choice Experiments

The section begins with an introduction explaining what choice experiments are along with typical examples. Next, we give an application illustrating use of DCEs in health economics. Following that, we discuss DCEs in core experimental economics, the pros and cons of DCEs, social desirability issues, and the problem of hypothetical bias. This is followed by a discussion of the key numerical choices that need to be made: number of choice sets, number of options in a choice set, number of attributes, number of levels. The *random utility model* (RUM) (and RPM) are the workhorses of discrete choice data analysis. The latent class model is also useful and we give examples with a focus on designing and modelling; in the example for choosing health insurance, the latent class model is used and, when the classes have been learned, classes are then described in terms of socio-economic covariates.

This section is strongly linked to the section on optimal design, since the examples typically use D-optimality (or its Bayesian counterpart) to determine the experimental design. While the 'general theory' can accommodate a situation with K possible responses for each question (for K finite), the questions usually present two or three options (option A, option B, refuse both). The most common model is the RPM (a variant of the RUM). Another popular model is the *latent class model*. Latent simply means *hidden* and the *latent class model* (LCM) simply infers a finite set of classes (or categories) from observations and assigns observations to these classes. Section 4.9.2 presents an interesting use of both the RPM and the LCM. Individuals express their preferences between various options for health insurance. Analysing the data according to the RPM suggests heterogeneity in the parameters. At the same time, the subjects are asked questions about socio-economic variables and the LCM is employed to learn classes which explain the heterogeneity of parameters in the RPM. The idea is to determine how the socio-economic category is related to preferences for health insurance.

4.1 What Are Choice Experiments?

Discrete choice experiments (DCEs) are widely used in environmental economics and health economics. The name may be confusing from the viewpoint of an experimental economist because nearly all experiments in economics involve some choices. The term also conceals the fact that a very similar approach is used in other disciplines, notably marketing, where it is called 'conjoint analysis'.

Whatever the name, the essence of the method is that each subject faces a number of 'choice sets' involving decisions between two or more options. In the lingo of experimental economics, it is thus a case of a within-subject design. The options differ on a number of dimensions (called attributes). Different participants may face different blocks of choice sets: the attributes and levels used remain the same but the specific combinations comprising options and choice sets are different. For example, sixty choice sets may be used divided into five blocks, with each participant only going through one block of twelve choices. Let us have a look at a typical example of a choice experiment in the field of environmental economics.

Suppose you live in the west of Australia, a country well known for its weird fauna (which might have evolved to adjust to walking upside down). You are approached by researchers Subroy, Rogers, and Kragt (2018) who are concerned about endemic species of small marsupials: numbats, also known as walpurti [*sic*], and woylies, also known as brush-tailed bettongs [*sic*]. Both species, once roaming across the continent, are now critically endangered, with the wilderness of Dryandra Woodlands being one of their last strongholds. You are told it is mostly red foxes and feral cats that are to blame for this unfortunate course of events. Effective 'management' of these invasive predators in the Woodlands is the numbats' and woylies' only chance for survival. You are introduced to a number of possible strategies, such as fencing, trapping, and

	Option A (Primary management strategy)	Option B	Option C	Option D
Management strategy	1080 baiting	1080 baiting + Trapping	Fencing + Trapping + Community Engagement	Fencing
Numbat population in 5 years' time 	100	100	250	400
Woylie population in 5 years' time 	2,500	2,500	2,500	7,500
Annual cost to your household each year for the next 5 years	$0/year	$50/year	$400/year	$150/year

Figure 3 Choice experiment screenshot Subroy et al. (2018).

baiting (poisoning). You are told these strategies may involve yearly costs to be covered from the taxes paid by all Western Australia households. You are then asked to make six choices between four options each, such as the one represented in Figure 3.

As can be seen in the picture, there are four attributes: the strategy, the number of numbats, the number of woylies, and the cost. On each dimension, one of a few different levels may be taken into account. The attributes and its levels are informed by the menu of policy options that may actually be available and the preferences of the population that could be taken into account when actually choosing one of these options.

Typically, trade-offs arise between the attributes. For example, in Figure 3, Option C saves more numbats compared to Option B, but is more expensive. These trade-offs will be different in each choice set, saving numbats (or woylies) being cheap in some choice sets and expensive in others. By analysing your pattern of answers, the researchers will thus be able to calculate how much you are willing to pay to save one numbat or one woylie and perhaps if you have any sympathy for the predators. In this case, Subroy and colleagues (2018) found that a typical participant preferred combining different management strategies over the currently implemented baiting. They were also willing to pay about 21.76 AUD for 100 numbats and 7.95 AUD for 1,000 woylies. The researchers determined the second relationship by observing that increasing the cost of the option by about 7.95 AUD was, on average, equally detrimental to its popularity as reducing the woylie population by 1,000. This also meant that each numbat was worth some 25 woylies. The researchers also reported that these numbers did not depend on whether the photographs of the marsupials were shown, a condition randomised between subjects (although some googleable woylie images are seriously cute). As a side note, with nearly 1 million households in Western Australia and a typical numbat weighing just about 500 grams, this amounts to some 100,000 AUD per kilogram, making the price of Olive Wagyu or Kobe beef look very reasonable in comparison.

If you do not have the stomach to poison one fluffy beastie to save another, you may want to participate in a marketing study instead. While the content is very different and the researchers may call it an example of a 'choice-based conjoint analysis' rather than simply a choice experiment, the structure of the decision task is rather similar. For example, Toubia and colleagues (2007) would give you a choice between different wines. They would differ in terms of closure type (traditional cork, synthetic cork, Metacork, 7 Stelvin (screw cap)), type of wine (dry, aromatic, dry red, blush red), region of origin (Australia/New Zealand, France, Sonoma/Napa, Chile/Argentina), vintner (small boutique, midsize regionally known winery, large nationally recognized winery, international conglomerate winery) and, not surprisingly, the price range. Again, the sequence of choices between options, presented analogously to those of Figure 3, would allow the researchers to estimate the utility of each level.

4.2 Discrete Choice Experiments in Health economics: An Example

Health economics represents a domain in which choice experiments have been used extensively. Let us discuss an example of this literature, which shows some interesting features.

The aim of the study by Papoutsi and colleagues (2015) was to establish how fiscal-food policies (subsidies of healthy products and fat taxes) affected parents' choice of diet for their children. Thereby, they wanted to control for the children's 'pester power' – the ability to persuade the parents to buy tasty rather than healthy foods. For this reason, a between-subject manipulation was used. Half of the parents would go through the choice tasks with ('Pester'), the others without ('No Pester') the presence of the child. Of course, to ensure comparability of these groups, both were recruited in the same way and had to show up with the child. The experiment also varied information provision: the rationale of the food policies (subsidies and taxes) was revealed to the parents ('Info' treatment) or not ('No Info' treatment). For both dimensions, within-subject manipulation would have been problematic. In particular, it would have been relatively easy for the participants to guess the hypothesis if they answered only *some* questions with their children present. Likewise, it would have been impossible to have participants obtain and then immediately forget the information about the fiscal policies.

Participants were asked to make four choices between pairs of foods. Three attributes were considered: healthiness (less vs. more healthy), fat tax (present vs. absent), and subsidy (present vs. absent). Perhaps not surprising, the fat tax could be applied only to the unhealthy item and the subsidy only to the healthy one. It is fairly common in choice experiments (and thus possible to implement in software packages helping to design them) that some combinations are excluded. Here, burdening the healthy option only with a fat tax would not make much sense and analogously for the subsidy.

A feature that is *not* common was that the values of the attributes were not listed in a table. Instead, they were only revealed implicitly – participants could see the amended prices and judge the healthiness of the products themselves.

The main findings were as follows:

- Implementing a fat tax and a subsidy *simultaneously* results in a significant, positive interaction.
- Providing information regarding the fiscal-food policies can further increase the impact of the intervention.
- Child pestering strongly moderates the effectiveness of the policies; it is a heavy influence on the choices that parents make that leads them to unhealthier choices.

Again, compared to a basic design (experimental group vs. control group), combining different dimensions in a single choice experiments facilitated comparing main effects and identifying interactions.

4.3 Choice Experiments in Core Experimental Economics

Choice experiments can be put to good use outside the domains in which they are well established, namely environmental economics and health economics. One subfield in which this is happening is the study of attitudes towards inequality between one's own income and the income of others. For example, Shigeoka and Yamada (2019) first asked their UK- and US-based responders to whose income they are likely to compare their own (family members, former classmates, general population etc.). Subsequently, they instructed them to make a series of hypothetical choices between pairs of situations (allowing for indifference). Each situation was characterised by two attributes: one's own income and the reference group's income. The possible levels corresponded to quantiles of the distribution of actual pre-tax monthly income levels in the relevant country, ranging from 900 USD (700 GBP) to 7,200 USD (5,500 GBP) in the US (UK). This is quite different from the more common method of investigating preference for the incomes of others (or, alternatively, for one's own *relative* income). The latter would involve eliciting subjective well-being or, more narrowly, satisfaction with one's own income as well as that of some reference group (which, along with many control variables, would become a regressor). Arguably, the key difference is that for this traditional approach, the focus is on the level of utility actually *experienced* by an individual facing given circumstances. By contrast, in DCEs, we hope to elicit *decision* utility driving choices between different sets of circumstances. To the extent that people may systematically mispredict the determinants of their happiness, these two approaches just measure two different things and need not be in sync.

The traditional approach also has some characteristics which should better be thought of as bugs rather than features and which can be avoided if a choice experiment is run. In the choice experiment, variables of interest (own and others' income) are directly observable; they can be exogenously manipulated to take several different values (rather than be fixed, endogenous, and measured with error as in the standard approach); the estimates are much more comparable across cultures and languages than in the case of elicitation of home-grown subjective well-being measures. Using choice experiments here also has advantages over alternative experimental designs (typically manipulating just one variable) as discussed in Section 4.4.

In Clark, Senik, and Yamada (2017), the authors were able to compare the results of a choice experiment with those of the traditional survey-based approach. In a large online study conducted in Japan, they included two modules. The first module followed the traditional approach. The responders were asked, 'About how much do you suppose was the average personal income (before taxes) in 2009, for people of the same age, sex, and education as you?'. They were also asked about their own income and how satisfied they were with it. The second module included a hypothetical choice experiment in which one's own and one's peer group's incomes were exogenously manipulated. Interestingly, the two approaches led to rather similar conclusions, greatly reinforcing their reliability.

The study of Cetre and colleagues (2019) is an example of a choice experiment on relative income in which the choices could actually be implemented. This is because it concerned low one-time payments in a group of five (rather than wages relative to a wide peer group). The authors manipulated the source of inequality (based on luck vs. based on performance) and whether the choice was made before or after the positions were known. Overall, they found little support for the importance of relative income, with large majority of subjects endorsing Pareto-superior distributions even if they reduced their own income relative to that of the others.

On top of preference for relative income, choice experiments were occasionally employed in a wide range of other topics in experimental economics. For example, Steimle and colleagues (2022) investigated the determinants of willingness to return to the campus (rather than postpone it) during the Covid-19 pandemic. The choice of attributes and their levels was informed by the recommendations that the US universities had obtained from the Centers for Disease Control and Prevention. A typical decision screen showing all the attributes included is exhibited in Figure 4. A DCE is an appealing design choice for a number of reasons. Firstly, a decision like this is indeed likely to hinge on a number of dimensions which can be reflected as attributes of a choice experiment. Secondly, several of these attributes are nominal variables taking a few distinct levels, which naturally fits a DCE. Thirdly, they may interact; for example, regulations concerning masks may be more important when classes are conducted in person. Identifying these interactions would not have been possible if each dimension had been studied separately. Fourthly, the decisions made by students are unprecedented. It would have thus likely been difficult for them to express their preference in an abstract manner, whereas it was easier to make choices between specific combinations. Fifthly (and related), ex ante,

Among the following options, which one do you prefer?

	Enroll in Option 1	Enroll in Option 2	Option 3 (Defer)
Mode of course delivery	All classes entirely online	All classes deliver large lectures online & small group activities in-person	Defer enrollment for at least one term
Safety on Campus	No masks & no COVID-19 testing	Masks required & some COVID-19 testing	
Residence Hall Operating Capacity	Closed, 0% capacity	Open, 100% capacity	
Tuition Reduction	10%	30%	
Limits on Events and Social Gatherings	No limit	20 people	

	Enroll in Option 1	Enroll in Option 2	Defer Enrollment (Option 3)
Your choice:	●	○	○

Figure 4 Choice experiment screenshot Steimle et al. (2022).

not only the relative sizes of the effect of different dimensions were unclear, but also their directions. For example, it cannot be excluded that some students preferred strict restrictions on the permitted size of gatherings. A choice experiment enables identification of such cases. Finally, it should be noted that some campus rules could send a signal about the seriousness of the pandemic conditions: severity of restrictions could be perceived as indicative of the severity of the situation. In a between-subject design, this could lead to a paradoxical situation in which a student who is highly concerned about safety is less willing to return to the campus when the restrictions are more severe. This is because these strict regulations would send them a signal that the pandemic situation is serious. A choice experiment in which a whole range of different sets of restrictions is presented reduces the probability of such an artefact; participants are likely to understand that they should assume that all of the possible choice determinants that are *not* listed on the screen stay constant.

As before, one of the attributes – in this case the tuition reduction – was of monetary nature. This allowed a direct estimation of the WTP for various campus Covid-policy changes.

4.4 Pros and Cons of Choice Experiments

The same problem of estimating WTP could be addressed more directly using open questions. The participants may be asked about the maximum amount they would pay (in terms of tuition in the case of Covid-19 restrictions at the campus, in terms of taxes in the case of environmental protection policies, etc.). Such open-ended contingent valuation methods were used extensively in the past. By now, they have been largely replaced by DCEs. One reason for this switch is that open questions tend to trigger a lot of zero responses and, at the same time, a large number of unreasonably high responses. Naturally, it may well be that some people indeed have zero WTP for certain (environmental) public goods; likewise, it may be difficult to tell if a response is indeed 'unreasonable'. Nevertheless, the consensus in the community is that many of these cases are artefacts of the cognitive difficulty of coming up with a specific number. By contrast, choosing between two or three options tends to be easier. This shift parallels development in some subfields of experimental economics. For example, in decisions under risk, direct valuation of gambles is nowadays rarely used; utility is instead inferred from choices between gambles. On top of cognitive difficulty considerations, a bonus gain is that one can directly incentivise choices, whereas incentivising valuations requires methods such as the Becker–DeGroot–Marschak (BDM). Such methods are often criticised; we discuss some problems with the BDM method in Section 5.5.3.

Problems with incentivisation also arise in non-choice-based conjoint analysis in marketing. Here, the traditional approach is that each option (characterised by different attributes) is presented separately; the subject indicates on a scale, of say, 0 to 100, the level of personal liking of the product or the likelihood that the subject would buy it. Again, even if all versions of the product are available, there is no obvious and direct way to incentivise statements such as 'I'd buy this product with a probability of 65 per cent' and the well-known ways of incentivising probabilistic predictions, such as proper scoring rules, do not apply to situations where the forecaster can actually easily affect the outcome.

4.5 Hypothetical Bias: Incentivising Choice Experiments

Sticking to standard choice experiments does not necessarily help address the problem of incentive compatibility. Indeed, in both choice experiments and conjoint analysis in marketing, the choices are typically hypothetical. This may give rise to a discrepancy between hypothetical responses and those that would have been given if responders were incentivised to reveal true preference. Such a hypothetical bias may arise due to many reasons. Participants may fail to take hypothetical questions seriously; they may be tempted to answer quickly, without careful examination of the situation and their preference. This is likely to be the case when the decision problem is complex. Secondly, the problem may be aggravated when some options appear more socially acceptable, morally superior, or more fashionable than others. Participants may then want to misrepresent their preference. For example, when considering desirable features of a product, people may want to signal that they value 'organic' more highly than they actually do. They may also actually believe that they value it highly, even if this is not really reflected in their choices.

Of course, some choice experiments involve choices between options that *can* be implemented easily. For example, Buckell, White, and Shang (2020) ran a choice experiment with current smokers who have also used e-cigarettes in the past. They were asked to make choices between traditional cigarettes and vapes differing in terms of their health consequences, flavour, and price (with the option of abstaining always available). Before they started, the randomly chosen half of the subjects were told they would receive 100 USD worth of their preferred merchandise (from among one randomly selected choice set) at the end of the experiment. They were thus incentivised to choose in accordance with their genuine preference, while the choices were merely hypothetical for the remaining participants. While this was feasible, giving away (or selling) cigarettes under the disguise of science was certainly something that needed serious consideration of the relevant institutional review board or ethics committee.

Needless to say, such an approach may be implemented in choice-experiment-like designs studying more typical behavioural economics issues, such as other-regarding preferences. We would give the participant a number of choice sets involving options differing in terms of payments for oneself and others and simply implement the option chosen by the participant from a randomly selected choice set.

In many applications, however, the choices do not involve private goods, but rather community-level policies (e.g. how to kill some foxes in the most optimal way), and it is thus not possible to reward each subject directly with their most preferred option. Environmental economists often deal with this by trying to orchestrate 'consequentiality' (Vossler and Evans 2009). The idea is that participants may be led to believe that their responses could eventually affect actual policy choices.

Arguably, it requires a major leap of faith to conclude that this is anything similar to incentive compatibility that we have in typical lab experiments. Firstly, participants may doubt that study results will be looked at at all. Secondly, even if they do, some policies featured in it such as zero-cost policies other than the status quo may be unimplementable. Please note, by the way, that it may still make a lot of sense to include them, because they help estimate the importance of different dimensions. Thirdly, it seems plausible that said policies may be further modified before implementation, perhaps not to the participant's liking. Fourthly, except for the case of a single binary question, it may be optimal to distort true preferences. Suppose, for example, that respondents are given the choice between options A, B, and C and the most popular of them is going to be implemented. If one can expect that C is going to be unpopular, whereas A and B have a chance, then it is individually rational to choose the most preferred from among these two, even if C is actually preferred Vossler, Doyon, and Rondeau (2012). This is akin to strategic voting in first-past-the-post elections, resulting, for example, in very few votes for candidates not endorsed by either of the two main parties in US presidential elections.

4.6 Social Desirability

The fact that we cannot immediately observe the effect of any attribute taken individually has another positive aspect to it, due to *social desirability* bias and related effects. When *several* attributes are involved in a study, it is more difficult for the participants to guess what the hypotheses are. Even if they can guess, they may be less inclined to hide their preferences because they are not so obviously on display. Suppose, for example, that somebody does not care about the environmental impact at all, but recognises that such an attitude may not be widely appreciated. Because the design manipulates *several* dimensions, it may not be immediately obvious from the patterns of the responses that environmental impact considerations do not change the subject's choices.

In a recent DCE in which one of us was involved (Krawczyk et al. 2023), European respondents indicated their willingness to support a policy of temporary protection of hypothetical groups of future migrants characterised by attributes such as fraction of children among them, country of origin, religious background, or reason for displacement (economic reasons, climate change, war). After they made their choices, we asked them directly how important each of these attributes was. Comparing these two types of responses, we realised that variation on some dimensions, notably migrants' religious background, affected participants' choices in the DCE to a much greater extent than they were willing to admit. Apparently many people were hesitant to welcome Muslim migrants and their DCE choices reflected this preference. By contrast, they were not willing to admit it when asked explicitly.

Even more direct evidence that DCE can help overcome social desirability bias (SDB) comes from a recent study by Horiuchi, Markovich, and Yamamoto (2022) (which also discusses the use of DCEs in political science). These authors compared preferences concerning a sensitive issue (e.g. whether the respondent would vote for a congressional candidate involved in a case of sexual harassment) elicited in two ways. The first was a standard DCE, in which the attribute of interest (AoI) was hidden among several others. In the second design, only the AoI was manipulated; other attributes were kept constant. Only in the second design was the extent to which participants reacted (or not) to candidates' involvement in sexual harassment transparent (and participants knew it).

Then again, this intervention could have an effect beyond and above SDB; in particular, it is likely that this attribute received more attention, regardless of whether it was sensitive. The authors ran additional comparisons to disentangle this effect from SDB. For example, for non-sensitive attributes, one would expect no SDB, so the entire difference (i.e., the difference between the estimates obtained in a standard DCE and the design in which only the target dimension was manipulated) could be attributed to the difference in attention. Using a difference-in-differences approach, they could thus estimate the effect of SDB. The results they obtained suggested that SDB effect can be as high as about two-thirds of the true effect of the level of the sensitive attribute itself.

4.7 Key Numerical Choices to Make

Conducting a choice experiment requires setting a few numbers right. These include the number of choice sets in a block, the number of options in each choice set, the number of attributes, and the levels of each attribute. While separate considerations apply to each, they are interrelated.

A *choice set* is simply a subset of all of the available options; it is also referred to as a *question*; the subject chooses one of the alternatives in the choice set. A choice set has the following elements:

- Alternatives: A number of hypothetical alternatives.
- Attributes: The *attributes* of the alternatives.
- Levels: Each attribute has a number of possible *levels* or values that the attribute may take.

4.7.1 The Number of Choice Sets

Because every choice is inherently random, the key advantage of including more choice sets in a block is that it raises precision of estimation. Naturally, a larger number of choices is necessary when the number of attributes and/or levels per attribute is also large. Another consideration is whether the researcher is interested in interactions between different attributes; if so, more choices will typically be needed. Likewise, if substantial heterogeneity of participants is expected or if we need to estimate parameters at the individual level (rather than for a 'representative' participant), the blocks must be longer.

Then again, with too many choice sets, respondents can eventually become inattentive or drop out. Clearly, the decision will depend on the mode of collecting data: one can have more choice sets in the lab, fewer online; more with a sample of accountants, fewer with a sample of teenagers diagnosed with ADHD; more when the participants are sufficiently rewarded. Most DCEs have ten or fewer choices – although Czajkowski, Giergiczny, and Greene (2014) had as many as twenty-six and did not observe a decline in data quality. A longer discussion of pros and cons of within-subject designs, to which typical choice experiment belongs, was provided in Section 2.5.

4.7.2 The Number of Options in a Choice Set

Practical limitations are of importance here: how many options can fit on the screen? This number may be just two if we want to design a mobile-friendly online survey and it is difficult to label each level with one or two words. Assuming we can have more options, we need to decide how many. Three options, one of which may be understood as a 'status quo' in which nothing changes, is a popular choice. While to the practitioners it may feel about right in most cases, overall the findings concerning the impact of the number of options on the estimates seem to be mixed; see section 3.1.2 of Mariel et al. (2021).

4.7.3 The Number of Attributes

Just as for the number of options, the number of attributes may be restricted by what can be comfortably seen on the screen. Moreover, both dimensions of the table to be shown to the participant – the number of options and the number of attributes – should be considered jointly in the context of the participant's cognitive capacity. In practice, it is rare to have more than five attributes. Then again, Meyerhoff, Oehlmann, and Weller (2015) observed no drop in data quality when the number of attributes increased from four to seven. Clearly, however, we cannot readily extrapolate this observation to any application; handling seven distinct dimensions can be very difficult in some (unfamiliar) domains, when there are too many options to choose from etc.

4.7.4 The Choice of Levels

The choice of the number of levels on each attribute and what these levels should specifically be is mostly dictated by the research question at hand and expected estimates. If we expect non-linear effects and it is important to detect them, then, obviously, more than two levels must be included. This is of particular importance when we may suspect the non-monotonic impact of some attribute (an internal optimum).

The choice of specific levels should typically be informed by what values are realistic or interesting from the viewpoint of applications. Another consideration is the anticipated strength of the effect. If the researcher expects some attribute to play a very large role, then the range of levels should be small or else it will be difficult to detect any effect of the other attributes. Clearly, it is advisable to consult experts in the subject matter and run pilot studies to make the best choice possible.

4.8 Designing Experiments and Modelling Data

4.8.1 Introduction

The distinctive feature of choice experiments, compared to typical experiments in economics, namely that we manipulate several dimensions at the same time, also has important consequences for statistical inference. Our objective is to identify the impact of different attributes, how the fact that an option is characterised by a specific level of a specific attribute affects the probability that it is selected. Because different choice sets differ in terms of several attributes, we cannot look at the simple summary statistics, which would be informative if there were only one change. Consider the simplest possible scenario of binary choices between a policy and the status quo. If Policy A, characterised by some combination of levels of various attributes, is preferred over the status quo 40 per cent of the time, and Policy A', which differs from Policy A on only one attribute, is chosen over the status quo 70 per cent of the time, we could conclude that the change from A to A' made the policy more attractive. Because there is only one difference between the two, it is this attribute that has made the difference. Such direct inference is generally not possible in choice experiments, because several attributes are manipulated simultaneously (and, typically, their levels change in more than one option). To estimate the effect of each attribute, parametric assumptions must thus be made.

It is fair to say that many experimental economists have a natural dislike of parametric methods. One reason is that they are aware of artefacts of arbitrary modelling choices aimed at obtaining attractive publishable results. The practice of preregistration of the methods of analysis and presentation of several specifications may, to some extent, alleviate these concerns. One seemingly positive aspect of the parametric approach is that the researcher explicitly models noise and this consideration informs design. Naturally, experimenters often team up with an expert when modelling choice-experimental data.

4.8.2 Random Utility and Related Models

We feel that we cannot add much to the excellent description of the RUM and several important variants found in Croissant (2020); the RUM where the utility in choice situation i of choice j is:

$$U_{ij} = V_{ij} + \epsilon_{ij}$$

where

$$V_{ij} = \alpha_j + \boldsymbol{\beta}'\boldsymbol{x}_{ij} + \boldsymbol{\nu}'\boldsymbol{t}_j + \boldsymbol{\gamma}_j' z_i + \boldsymbol{\delta}_j' \boldsymbol{w}_{ij}; \tag{4.1}$$

the covariates are:

- $\boldsymbol{x}_{ij}$ specific to the choice situation/alternative combination (i, j), with generic coefficients $\boldsymbol{\beta}$ and covariates $\boldsymbol{t}_j$ specific to the alternative j with a generic coefficient $\boldsymbol{\nu}$.
- Choice situation specific covariates z_i with alternative specific coefficients γ_j.

- Alternative and choice situation specific covariates $\boldsymbol{w}_{ij}$ with alternative specific coefficients $\boldsymbol{\delta}_j$.

Note that V_{ij} is a *linear* function of observable covariates and unknown parameters, which are to be estimated (see Croissant 2020 for details). In Section 5, we'll see that the *adaptive* designs of Chapman and colleagues (2018) and Toubia and colleagues (2013) allow for prospect theory utility functions, which have weighted probabilities and parameters which model loss aversion and risk aversion. It turns out (as pointed out in Croissant 2020) that the Gumbel distribution provides a convenient distribution for the error terms and the probability of choosing alternative j is:

$$\mathbb{P}_j = \frac{e^{V_j}}{\sum_{j=1}^{J} e^{V_j}}.$$

Croissant (2020) go on to describe the *heteroscedastic logit model*, where the errors are Gumbel, but no longer with the same parameters, the *nested* logit model and the *random parameters logit model* (RPLM).

The text of Croissant (2020) gives a full and user-friendly description of the RPLM. It is a popular model among practitioners, who find that it gives improved results over the RUM (this was the conclusion in both the examples of Section 4.9). While the standard RUM has the probability of a randomly chosen subject choosing alternative l in choice situation i as:

$$\mathbb{P}_{il} = \frac{\exp\{\boldsymbol{\beta}'\boldsymbol{x}_{il}\}}{\sum_j \exp\{\boldsymbol{\beta}'\boldsymbol{x}_{ij}\}},$$

where the parameters $\boldsymbol{\beta}$ are the same for *each* subject (and have to be estimated), the RPLM allows some variation. If we have n subjects, we take $\boldsymbol{\beta}_1, \ldots, \boldsymbol{\beta}_n$, the parameters for the respective subjects, as IID draws from a distribution, say (for example) $N(\boldsymbol{\beta}^{(0)}, C)$, where the parameters $\boldsymbol{\beta}^{(0)}$ and C have to be estimated. The covariance matrix C provides a measure of *heterogeneity*, – that is, the spread of $\boldsymbol{\beta}$ parameters between subjects. The package **mlogit** permits several distributions (e.g. normal, log normal, truncated normal). If the parameter vector is of length p where p is large (so that C has $\frac{1}{2}p(p+1)$ entries), we can restrict to C diagonal (assuming the different parameters are independent of each other) (details in Croissant 2020).

It is to be emphasised, therefore, that an optimal design for the RPLM will increase the ability to detect heterogeneity, since it will include the parameters of C (or at least the diagonal elements) which express the variation in the parameters between individuals. At the same time, though, for $\boldsymbol{\beta}$ a p-vector, then there are at least p *additional* parameters required (for parameter variances) if heterogeneity is suspected and hence more data is needed for accurate estimation, even with an optimal design.

4.8.3 Latent Class Model

We give more details about the LCM, since it is not described in Croissant (2020). It is, however, implemented in the package **apollo** (Hess and Palma 2019), a package which has many other useful implementations for choice experiments (including RUM, RPLM). The **apollo** website has a very useful collection of examples. The LCM for discrete choice analysis is an alternative method to the RPLM. The LCM for discrete choice analysis assumes a finite number of categories; for each category there is a 'true' parameter vector $\boldsymbol{\beta}$ and each individual belongs to one of these categories. This makes it less flexible than the RPLM, where each individual can have different parameters, but it is clearly more useful when it is important to locate the sources of the heterogeneity for individual preferences.

The LCM groups respondents in a finite number of classes (the number of classes may be chosen by analysing models with different numbers of classes and then using one of the standard selection criteria, such as the Akaike Information Criterion (AIC) or the Bayesian Information Criterion (BIC)). Membership of a specific class is based on the subject's answers to the DCE questions posed and also other characteristics (e.g. socio-demographic factors). The LCM assumes that the preferences of respondents are homogeneous within each class; they may be heterogeneous across classes. Grouping respondents with homogeneous preferences in a finite number of classes is relevant for decision makers because it helps them to understand the sources of heterogeneity between individuals.

The LCM works as follows: We place a prior probability of H_{iq}, that individual i is from class q, where $q \in \{1, \dots, Q\}$ and there are Q classes. The probability that individual i in choice set t chooses option j *given* that the individual is from class q is $\mathbb{P}_{it|q}(j)$ where $j \in \{1, \dots J\}$ (choice set has J alternatives). Here

$$\mathbb{P}_{it|q}(j) = \frac{\exp\{\boldsymbol{x}'_{it.j}\boldsymbol{\beta}_q\}}{\sum_{j=1}^{J}\exp\{\boldsymbol{x}'_{it.j}\boldsymbol{\beta}_q\}}.$$

The log-likelihood function for *all* the respondents is:

$$\log L = \sum_{i=1}^{N}\log\left\{\sum_{q=1}^{Q}H_{iq}\left(\prod_{t=1}^{T}\mathbb{P}_{it|q}(j)\right)\right\}.$$

A convenient and standard choice of prior H is a multinomial logit:

$$H_{iq} = \frac{\exp\{z_i'\boldsymbol{\theta}_q\}}{\sum_{p=1}^{Q} \exp\{z_i'\boldsymbol{\theta}_p\}} \qquad q = 1, \ldots Q, \quad \theta_Q = 0.$$

Here, z_i denotes a set of observable characteristics (e.g. socio-demographics such as age, income, and sex) that enter the model for class membership.

The parameters to be estimated are now the $\boldsymbol{\beta}_q$ parameters and also the $\boldsymbol{\theta}_q$ parameters. Once these have been estimated, the Bayes rule may be used to obtain respondent-specific (posterior) estimates of the class probability $\widehat{H}_{q|i}$, conditioned on their estimated choice probabilities:

$$\widehat{H}_{q|i} = \frac{\widehat{\mathbb{P}}_{i|q}\widehat{H}_{iq}}{\sum_{p=1}^{Q} \widehat{\mathbb{P}}_{i|p}\widehat{H}_{ip}}.$$

These respondent-specific (posterior) estimates of the class probability may then used in a *beta regression* analysis to profile the members of each class. To determine the number of classes, the Consistent Akaike Information Criterion (CAIC), and the BIC may be used.

After deciding on the number of classes and classifying respondents, each class may be characterised using, among other things, information on the attitudes and socio-demographic characteristics of respondents. Those variables may then be regressed against respondent-specific (posterior) estimates of the class probability $\widehat{H}_{q|i}$. Since the dependent variable is in form of probability, a beta regression model for each segment may be used.

For the first example of Section 4.9 (Shopping for Pasta in Italy, Section 4.9.1), the RPM is used and the questions are chosen according to a D-optimal design. In Section 4.9.2, again the RPM is used and questions chosen according to an efficient design. Analysis of the data suggests heterogeneity. The participants were asked further socio-economic questions and, based on the answers, the LCM was used. This model was *more* informative, since it shed light on the heterogeneity revealed by analysing data using the RPM. The aim was to provide long-term healthcare bundles appropriate to the various socio-economic categories.

4.9 Examples with Focus on Design and Modelling

This section contains two examples, both of which use the RPLM with a design that is (approximately) D-optimal. The long-term care insurance contracts example also analysed the data using an LCM, which indicated that the heterogeneity revealed by the RPLM was due to socio-economic categories (and there was parameter homogeneity within these categories).

4.9.1 Case Study: Shopping for Pasta in Italy

This example illustrates the use of *Bayesian truth serum* (BTS) and *inferred valuation* to elicit truthful answers in an incentivised choice experiment, optimal design (Section 3) and the RPM for analysing the data. The RPM adds an extra Bayesian layer over the mixed logit model; a prior distribution is placed over the parameters.

The choice experiment is by Menapace and Raffaelli (2020) and the aim is to determine whether BTS and inferred valuation are effective methods for dealing with hypothetical bias. Much of the detail is taken verbatim from Menapace and Raffaelli (2020), since we would like to represent their study accurately. We describe the study in some detail because it is well thought out and illustrates clearly the issues that have to be taken into account. Their study indicates that both BTS and inferred valuation can reduce, but not completely eradicate, hypothetical bias.

The authors collected both *stated* and *revealed* preference data from a sample of grocery shoppers; the revealed preference shows the true preferences and comparison with stated preferences enables the hypothetical bias to be quantified. The focus in this experiment was on *socially desirable* preference – for example, something being 'organic.' The interventions used here would be unlikely to reduce hypothetical bias in the expression of preference for something which was socially neutral and only a matter of personal taste, with no externalities.

The details of the empirical study are as follows. A sample of Italian shoppers were intercepted at organic stores belonging to an organic grocery chain. The study protocol consisted of three parts:

1. a discrete choice experiment, providing the stated preference data;
2. recording shoppers' pasta purchases during that one shopping trip (providing the *revealed* preference data needed to estimate the *true* WTP); and
3. recording of socio-demographic information.

The product used in the study was *durum wheat organic pasta* in the form of 'penne rigate'. By choosing organic pasta from an organic store, the vast range of attributes relevant to the purchase decision is narrowed, the most popular pasta brands are avoided, and the group of customers in the study is more homogeneous.

Six *attributes* were considered; by 'desirable public' we mean positive externalities:

Attribute	Nature	Levels
Guaranteed fair price paid to farmers	Desirable public	Present, Not present
Employment of disadvantaged people	Desirable public	Present, Not present
Processed with renewable energy	Desirable public / Undesirable private	Present, Not present
100% Italian	Desirable public and private	Present, Not present
Produced from ancient varieties	Desirable public and private	Present, Not present
Slow dried	Desirable private	Present, Not present
Price (euros / 500 g package)		1.19, 1,69, 2.19, 2.69, 3.19, 3.69

Describing 'renewable energy' as *undesirable private* may seem odd; it generally has positive associations as an environmental dimension of sustainability and is seen as a way to avoid the adverse environmental impacts of use of fossil fuels. As Menapace and Raffaelli point out, though, Italian consumers tend to hold renewable energy responsible for the price increase for agricultural raw materials (cereals in particular) and, consequently, the price increase for pasta. This amounts to a negative private connotation of renewable energy. Therefore, 'renewable energy' is the only attribute that combines desirable and non-desirable aspects.

Customers were presented with a *choice card*, each giving three alternatives: two product profiles and a no-buy option. Each choice card was associated with a direct or indirect question. For example, one card gave the choices found in Figure 5.

At this point, participants were randomly allocated to one of three treatments. In each treatment, 30 per cent of participants would obtain a coupon worth thirty euros, but the way the coupons were distributed depended on the treatment.

- **Control (CT)** In the control treatment, the thirty-euro coupons were allocated at random, therefore the monetary incentives were not connected with any move to encourage participants to state their *true* preferences; this

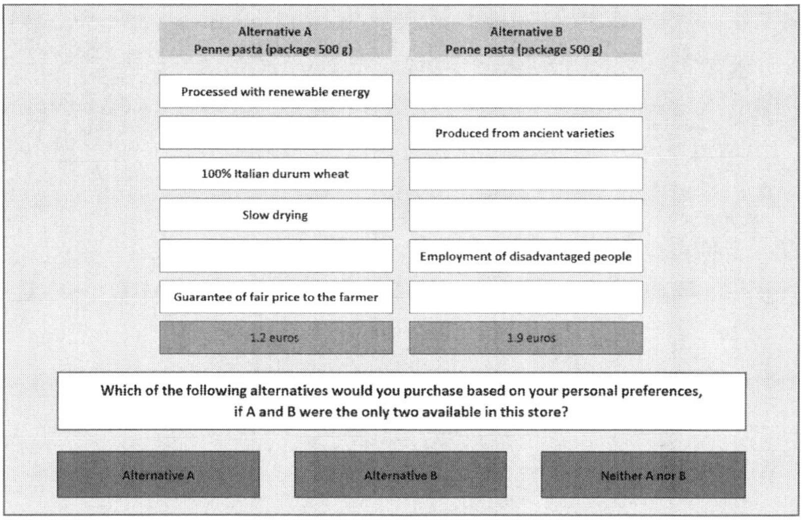

Figure 5 Choice experiment screenshot Menapace and Raffaelli (2020).

aspect simply indicated whether the existence of money changed the behaviour. For CT, only the question about the participant's *own* preference was asked.

- **Bayesian Truth Serum (BTS)** Participants were asked both the direct question about their own preference (choose between either A or B or none) and the indirect question about what they believed the preference of others would be when faced with the same choice: Alternative A, Alternative B, or none (giving their estimate of the proportion of customers in each category). Coupons were assigned to the top 30 per cent of respondents with the highest BTS scores.
- **Inferred Valuation Treatment (IV)** The thirty-euro coupons were assigned randomly. Respondents were *only* asked to judge the percentages of customers who would opt for Alternative A, Alternative B, or refuse to buy; no monetary incentives were offered to encourage the participants to reveal their actual beliefs.

When asked to assess the choices that *other* customers would make, the respondents were presented with the same options A and B. The respondents were asked to judge the percentage of customers who would opt for these three available options.

To refine the study of BTS, two further groups were assessed:

- The same set-up as BTS, except that only the *prediction score* was used when determining the 30 per cent of participants who were given coupons.

- The same set-up as BTS (both questions asked), except that coupons were assigned randomly (no incentives).

Designing the Experiment The authors used a Bayesian D-optimal design. Pretests and a pilot study (eighty interviews) were carried out to estimate prior probabilities for the experimental design and the final design for the main study was a D-efficient block design based on the information obtained in the pilot and pretests.

Empirical Specification Here, the utility that the respondent i experiences when selecting the pasta alternative j at time/occasion t is modelled by an RUM:

$$U_{ijt} = \alpha_i p_j + X_j' \beta_i + \epsilon_{ijt},$$

where, as the structure of an RUM dictates, the ϵ_{ijt}'s are independent identically distributed Gumbel random variables. p_j is the price of option j, X_j is the vector of attributes of option j (excluding price), and β_i is the vector of parameters for participant i.

4.9.2 Case Study: Long-Term Care Insurance Contracts

We now turn to an example which illustrates a situation where the LCM provides a distinct advantage. The DCE aims to elicit preferences for long-term care insurance (LTCI), where for each choice two bundles at different prices are presented. In addition to the choices made, information on a large number of socio-economic variables was presented. The participants were therefore categorised according to their responses to the questions about LTCI and the various categories were then described in terms of the socio-economic variables. The study aimed to elicit the needs, preferences, and WTP for LTCI and to establish the association between LTCI preferences and socio-economic situation.

Akaichi, Costa-Font, and Frank (2020) present a study where performing a DCE seems the only way to overcome the within-subject difficulties of resetting the subject after each question. Previous studies indicated that for other survey experiments tackling the same problem, responses to subsequent questions were heavily influenced by the first question presented; there was a 'first question effect' which was not additive and which could not be removed when analysing the results. By presenting pairs of options in a suitably randomised order, the DCE methodology solved this problem.

Two DCEs on LTCI were designed and carried out and the data analysed. The experiments examined choices made by a large sample of 15,298 individuals in the United States with and without insurance. The valuation of a number of insurance attributes was studied. These attributes were:

- the daily insurance benefit,
- insurance coverage, and
- the compulsory and voluntary nature of the insurance policy design

alongside

- costs (insurance premium) and
- health requirements.

The data was analysed in two ways: firstly, using an RPLM to dicover the preferences of respondents and and their WTP for the various attributes; the RPM is clearly appropriate due to heterogeneity of choice responses (i.e. the choices of different respondents are governed by different $\boldsymbol{\beta}$ vectors).

While analysis of the data using RPL clearly shows this heterogeneity (through covariance of the posterior), it gave no information about the causes of heterogeneity. Therefore, the data were also analysed using the LCM demographic, socio-economic information and also measures of attitude from each participant were gathered in a debriefing session. Analysis using the LCM segmented the respondents into homogeneous groups based on these attributes.

Description of the Choice Experiment The DCE was part of a larger Long-Term Care Awareness and Planning Survey commissioned by the US Department of Health and Human Services to examine consumer preferences for specific features of individual LTCI policies (e.g. benefit levels, duration of coverage, sponsorship). The sample was made up of 24,878 non-institutionalised adults forty to seventy years of age. In total, 15,298 people responded to the survey, yielding a 61.5 per cent response rate. The survey contained a long list of question on attitudes towards long-term care, the answers to which should give a good understanding of potential demand for LTCI. Respondents completed two related sets of DCE questions about insurance plans. The questions involved six attributes:

- daily benefit amount,
- benefit period,
- elimination period (deductible),
- health requirements,
- type of insurer, and
- monthly premium.

The two sets of questions were called DCE1 and DCE2; DCE1 included only the attributes just listed and DCE2 additionally included an attribute of whether participation in the LTCI plan was voluntary or mandatory. Therefore, the value of a 'voluntary' insurance scheme could be identified from the responses to DCE2. Since DCE2 was more complete, the analysis was carried out using the data from DCE2.

The opt-out alternative was chosen in all the choice sets in DCE2 by 19 per cent of respondents; their responses were excluded from the data so they did not distort the responses of the other respondents.

The Experiment The DCE survey consisted of a choice section and a questionnaire. In the choice section, participants were successively provided with eight different choice sets and were repeatedly asked to choose one of three options: there were two different LTCI policies and an opt-out option. Each LTCI policy displayed five choice sets (DCE1) described in terms of the six attributes. The LTCI policies shown to respondents in the last three choice sets (DCE2) were described in terms of seven choice sets: the six attributes already present in DCE1 and additionally the attribute 'type of enrollment'.

The first dimension of benefit design studied, in addition to the premium, was the so-called daily benefit. Other important dimensions were the type of insurer (public/private) and the type of enrollment (voluntary/compulsory).

Optimal Design There were 6 attributes in DCE1, giving $2^6 = 64$ possible policies. For each question, the subject was presented with a pair of policies; there were $\binom{64}{2} = 32\times63 = 2{,}016$ possible pairs. For DCE2 there were $2^7 = 128$ possible combinations of attributes and hence 8,128 possible pairs. Clearly, it is unwise to ask a subject to sit long enough to make 2,016 choices. The article states that 'the optimal design was drawn to minimise the standard errors of the parameter estimates (i.e., marginal utilities for the various insurance attributes)'; such a statement could correspond either to A-optimality (minimising the sum of the variances) or to D-optimality (minimising the determinant of the covariance) (see Section 3 for a discussion of alphabet optimality). Since it is not the parameters themselves that are in view, but rather estimates of the WTP coefficients, we would recommend a C-optimal design, where optimisation is with respect to variances of the WTP coefficient estimates.

The final design consisted of 500 unique choice questions (i.e. designs which repeated the same question were avoided), and they were split into 100 blocks of five choice questions each initially for DCE1. For the additional questions, 300 unique choice questions were broken into 100 blocks of three choice sets each.

Thus, each respondent was first asked to complete five choice questions, then given information about the seventh attribute ('type of enrollment') and asked to answer three more choice questions. In each choice set, respondents were asked to mark the alternative they preferred most (i.e. Policy A, Policy B, or no insurance), and within each block, the choice sets were randomly ordered. Furthermore, the A/B policies were randomly ordered between left and right sides of the screen.

In addition to responding to the eight choice questions, respondents were asked to answer several debriefing questions, which enabled the subjects to be categorised into homogeneous groups. The debriefing questions were asked to collect information on the following issues:

- Risk of needing long-term care,
- Psychological characteristics,
- Knowledge,
- Skills,
- Experience,
- Beliefs and concerns about long-term care,
- Retirement and long-term care planning,
- Information gathering and decision-making about insurance,
- Core demographic and socio-economic information, and
- Comparing insurance policies with a combination of features.

DCE Modelling The utility function for the RPL is (as usual):

$$U_{ijt} = \boldsymbol{\beta}'\boldsymbol{X}_{ijt} + \epsilon_{ijt},$$

where $\boldsymbol{\beta}$ is the vector of unknown utility parameters associated with the product attributes $\boldsymbol{X}_{ijt}$.

The variables corresponding to the attributes 'Daily Benefit', 'Deductible Period', and 'Monthly Premium Cost' were coded as continuous variables using their original values. For each of the rest of the attributes, zero-sum constraints were employed; $L - 1$ dummy variables were generated, where L is the number of levels of the attribute. The Lth level of each attribute was omitted to avoid the problem of multicollinearity. The omitted levels '1 year', 'Healthy and not Disabled', 'Federal Government', and 'Universal Plan' corresponding to the attributes 'Benefit Period', 'Health Requirements', 'Type of Insurer', and 'Type of Enrollment', respectively, were set as the baseline levels. Thus the estimated parameters represent the demand response of the respondents to the levels included with respect to the baseline level.

Summarising the Results The WTP coefficients were of importance; results from the estimation of the RPLM showed that attitudes of respondents were highly heterogeneous (as shown by diagnostics of the posterior over β). The RPLM enabled heterogeneity to be included, but (of course) could not explain the source of the heterogeneity.

Latent Class Model The RPLM showed existence of heterogeneity, but did not pinpoint the causes of heterogeneity, which are important for understanding attitudes towards LTCI. The LCM was used with the aim of assigning individuals to homogeneous classes, which may be described by the socio-demographic factors and the information obtained in the debriefing.

The prior H over classes used in this study was a multinomial logit:

$$H_{iq} = \frac{\exp\{\mathbf{z}_i'\boldsymbol{\theta}_q\}}{\sum_{p=1}^{Q} \exp\{\mathbf{z}_i'\boldsymbol{\theta}_p\}} \qquad q = 1, \ldots Q, \quad \theta_Q = 0,$$

where z_i denotes a set of observable characteristics (e.g. socio-demographics such as age, income, and sex, information obtained in the debriefing) and $q \in \{1, \ldots, Q\}$ denotes the class label.

5 Adaptive Designs

In this chapter we explore adaptive designs in which the stimuli are not pre-determined. Instead, subsequent questions depend on previous answers. We discuss how such ‘chaining’ can give substantial improvement to the efficiency of data collection, but also some of the challenges it creates, notably with incentivising choices (while maximising transparency and avoiding deception). Focusing on individual decision-making under risk, we discuss both non-parametric and parametric methods.

5.1 Introduction

The natural way to find out is to ask. Often, a single question is not sufficient and eliciting information is a *dynamic* process; answers to previous questions determine subsequent questions. This is why, when talking to a four-year-old, it is sometimes best not to give any answer at all, because whatever we say is bound to provoke another ‘why?’. Although some four-year-olds are exceptions, we do not usually ask questions we know will not be answered. Likewise, there is little point in asking questions to which we already know the answer (unless we are professors examining our students, or we are politicians radicalising the voters).

A good design could follow the same natural rules of communication. One research technique that clearly does this is an interview, where we only have a loose scenario and adjust our questions on the fly. This is very helpful, especially in exploratory research, but interviews clearly have their downsides.

Interviewing can be costly to implement. Also, the researcher may have an undue effect on the outcome; results may depend heavily on the skills as well as the preconceptions of the interviewer. This is not good, since we want research results which are replicable (and which remain the same for a variety of valid methods). Also, with an 'on the fly' approach, the researcher may be unable to come up with the optimal question to be posed next, on the spot. Therefore, especially when carrying out an experiment (rather than an exploratory pilot study), it is usually more practical to let the algorithms do their magic, choosing the next question from a predetermined list. In this chapter we overview some examples of how this can be done.

A note on the terminology may be in order here, since there are a few terms that are nearly synonymous which are used in this respect. Questions that depend on previous answers are sometimes referred to as being *chained* and, in other sources, *linked*. The design may be called *dynamic* or *adaptive*; these terms are used interchangeably.

5.1.1 Connection to Choice Experiments and Optimal Design

This section is a natural continuation of Section 4 whereby, instead of deciding on all the questions at the same time, we choose the questions sequentially; each question is chosen to give as much additional information as possible. The discussion of Lindley's SIG criterion, which we described in Section 3, is particularly pertinent here; with this criterion, the information from the experiment as a whole can be seen as the sum of the information gained in each successive part. When we construct a sequential design, the subsequent questions are likely to be different from each other, so that the assumption of independent answers for within-subject questioning is reasonable. Furthermore, this section represents a *progression* from Section 4; the RUM and its variants used in the examples in Section 4 are based on *linear* utilities, while for the adaptive designs of Chapman et al. (2018) and Toubia et al. (2013), probability weighting and utilities from prospect theory are incorporated.

5.1.2 Benefits

The key potential advantage of dynamic designs is that, compared with standard static designs, they allow us as researchers collect more information and/or take less of the subject's time. This is because we do not waste time asking questions that are unlikely to modify substantially the estimates of the parameters of the utility function. The additional advantage of avoiding such uninformative questions is that many of them would seem uninteresting also from the subject's point of view. That is particularly true for obvious questions where, from the viewpoint of a given subject, one option may be dramatically better than the other. Again, if it can be inferred from previous answers that a given question will be obvious for a given subject, a dynamic design may allow us to ask some other question instead.

Another possible advantage is that dynamic procedures allow the subjects to face a short series of easier tasks (e.g. answering binary questions) rather than a large, difficult task (e.g. matching). Since we avoid obvious questions *and* cognitively very demanding questions, there is a better chance that subjects will remain engaged and provide meaningful responses.

By formulating questions taking previous responses into account, response errors or violations of key assumptions can be accommodated *within* the experiment.

Finally, a typical feature of dynamic designs is that at least some parameters of the utility function are estimated in real time. This may be convenient, particularly when we want to provide some feedback to the subjects (e.g. for didactic purposes) and if we want to classify subjects immediately; for example, we may want endogenous matching in another behavioural task.

5.2 Problems and Challenges

Naturally, on-the-fly estimation also presents challenges. Programming the experiment may be trickier than with static designs and we may need computational power to ensure that subjects do not have to wait for the program to decide on the next question. Furthermore, adaptive designs may require additional or stronger assumptions and so be less robust to changes in functional forms. A question that is dynamically optimal based on one theory may be way off based on another theory. In this sense, a longer, static design may yield data that is more amenable to the whims of Reviewer 2 who requires (ex post, obviously) an analysis based on a completely different set of assumptions. Then again, an adaptive design could thus also be thought of as a commitment device, providing us with a good argument *not* to yield to the whims of Reviewer 2. In this sense, it plays a similar role to that of preregistration of design and analysis (but, naturally, an adaptive design can also be preregistered).

Similarly, a dynamic design many not be very robust in the face of mistakes. *Propagation of errors*, whereby misrepresentation of the preferences of subjects in early questions has serious bearing for the estimates obtained in subsequent questions, is a real possibility.

Also, the techniques available, as we shall see, are of a hierarchical Bayesian flavour which requires functional assumptions and distributional assumptions, both over the likelihood and prior, for all the hierarchical levels required.

Finally, incentive compatibility and the rule of avoiding deception usually require more scrutiny with dynamic designs than with standard static designs. This is because when answers determine future questions, it may not be optimal to answer truthfully (and we may be guilty of deception if we tell the subjects that it is optimal).

5.3 A Simple Example: Bisection and Iterated Multiple Price List

Suppose that almost for everyone, a widget is worth between €0 and €100. The simplest way to pin it down for a specific subject is of course to ask directly, 'How much is the widget worth to you?' (*matching*). This, though, is often a cognitively demanding question. Asking, say, nine questions 'Is the widget worth more than €10 / €20 / …/ €90 to you?' (nine *simple binary choice* questions) may be annoying and only gives us a €10 interval, not a point estimate. Asking 'Is the widget worth more than €50 to you?' and then 'Is it worth more than €25 / €75?' etc., depending on previous answers (*bisection*), makes for greater precision with just four questions (of which only the first one or two will tend to be obvious). The *iterative multiple price list* technique is analogous, except that the interval which should, in view of previous answers, cover the value of interest gets partitioned into more than two at each stage. The basic method is also known by other names, including titration and the staircase method.

In the simple application of the iterative multiple price list technique, incentive compatibility and deception may not be a large problem. If an iterated procedure yields €1 precision, it means that the subject has explicitly or implicitly answered questions 'Is the widget worth more than €x' for $x = 1, \ldots, 99$, so we can pick one of them at random and implement it. It is in subject's best interest to answer all questions truthfully.

Still, such a BDM approach has been criticised and justly so; Horowitz (2006) points out that when the declared maximum WTP is not based on simple expected utility, it is not necessarily equal to the actual WTP. He gives an example of *disappointment aversion*; the BDM approach is seen as a *game* with a probability distribution F over the price c. Let v be the declared maximal WTP and let $\tilde{c}(v)$ denote the *certainty equivalent price*. This is the price where, if the good were offered with certainty at that price, the utility of having the good, together with a remaining income of $Y - \tilde{c}(v)$ (where Y denotes the individual's total income), would be equivalent to the game. More formally, if $u(1,x)$ and $u(0,x)$ denote the respective utilities of having and not having the good, with income x, then $\tilde{c}(v)$ is the value that satisfies:

$$u(1, Y - \tilde{c}(v)) = \int_0^v u(1, Y - c)dF(c) + u(0, Y)(1 - F(v)).$$

The individual will be disappointed if $\tilde{c}(v) < c < v$ or if $c > v$ (and the individual does not get the good). If α and β are the respective weights attached to these disappointments, the expected utility for a declared WTP upper bound v is then:

$$\begin{aligned} U(v) = & \int_0^v u(1, Y - c)dF(c) + u(0, Y)(1 - F(v)) \\ & - \alpha \int_{\tilde{c}(v)}^v (u(1, Y - \tilde{c}(v)) - u(1, Y - c))dF(c) \\ & - \beta(u(1, Y - \tilde{c}(v)) - u(0, Y))(1 - F(v)). \end{aligned}$$

When $\alpha \neq 0$ or $\beta \neq 0$, the optimal value of v is not equal to the WTP upper bound in a situation where the participant was presented with the good at a fixed price on a take-it-or-leave-it basis.

5.4 Non-parametric Methods in the Context of Prospect Theory

More sophisticated dynamic designs have been used predominantly in the domain of decision-making under risk. Particularly when we allow for non-linear weighing of probabilities, comprehensive assessment of preference is a challenge. Suppose, for example, that someone is inclined to appreciate a gamble highly, even if it offers a low expected pay-off, as long as it gives a chance (albeit a small one) for a very high pay-off. It would seem to mean that this high pay-off is perceived as extremely attractive. In the framework of *cumulative prospect theory* (CPT) (Tversky and Kahneman 1992), it could also mean that it is given undue decision weight, much larger than its meager probability. For simplicity, we restrict our attention to gambles with two outcomes at most. Firstly, consider positive outcomes only. The CPT postulates the existence of a continuous, increasing probability weighting function (PWF) for gains, w^+ satisfying $w^+(0) = 0, w^+(1) = 1$ (see Figure 6).

The PWF determines decision weights of outcomes based not only on their probability, but also their (de)cumulative probability: every outcome receives a decision weight which, in general, not only deviates from its probability, but also depends on whether the other outcomes are better or worse. Specifically, in the case of a two-outcome non-negative gamble in which the highest outcome is obtained with probability p, its decision weight is $w^+(p)$, whereas the decision weight of the lowest outcome is $1 - w^+(p)$. This means that, for example, a concave w^+ function, yielding $w^+(p) > p$ for all ps, would give an undue

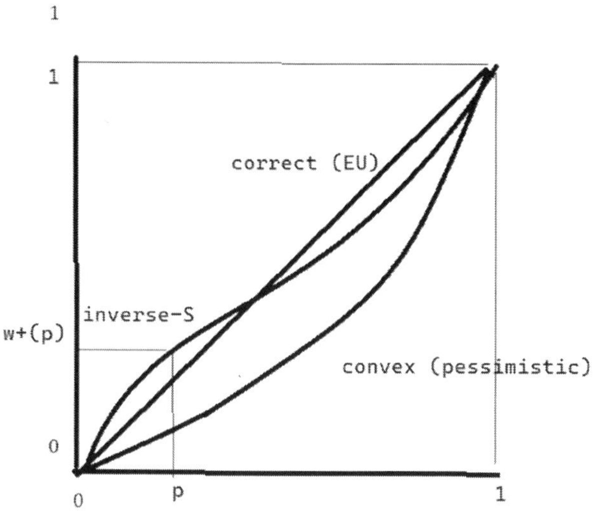

Figure 6 CPT probability weighting function.

weight to the highest outcome, pushing the decision maker toward risk seeking; note that this would not necessarily *make* the subject risk-seeking, because the shape of the utility function may work in the opposite direction.

One way to infer something about the shape of the utility function is to first elicit a sequence of outcomes equally spaced in terms of utility (aka standard sequence, Wakker and Deneffe 1996) – that is, such $x_0, x_1 \ldots, x_k$ that $U(x_i) - U(x_{i-1})$ is identical for all $i = 1, \ldots, k$. For a linear utility function, we would then have $x_1 - x_0 = x_2 - x_1$, etc. Under expected utility theory, risk aversion would result from a concave utility function, meaning that $x_i - x_{i-1} > x_j - x_{j-1}$ when $i > j$; each extra payment required to yield the same utility boost is larger than the previous one. Again, under CPT, the shape of the utility function alone does not determine risk posture.

To elicit the standard sequence, we make use of two *reference* outcomes $R > r > 0$. Fixing the first element of the sequence, $x_0 (> R)$ and probability p, we seek to find $s > x_0$ such that the gamble giving s with probability p and r otherwise, denoted $Right = (s, p; r, 1 - p)$, is as good as the reference gamble $Left = (x_0, p; R, 1 - p)$. We can do it by asking binary questions and adjusting the higher outcome s in *Right* upwards or downwards accordingly, as we did before, seeking WTP for widgets. For example, with $r =$ €10, $R =$ €20, $x_0 =$ €30 and $p = 0.25$, we can first ask the subject to choose between lotteries $Left = (30, 0.25; 20, 0.75)$ and $Right = (60, 0.25; 10, 0.75)$. Note that in *Right*, compared to *Left*, the higher outcome has been improved by €30, but the lower outcome, which is three times more likely to obtain, has been worsened by €10.

In terms of expected value, these changes balance each other out. Thus a risk-neutral subject will be indifferent. A subject who seriously overweights the relatively low probability of 0.25 may prefer *Right*. In other words, for such a subject *Right* is too good, because we are seeking to establish indifference. We may thus ask the subject to choose between the unchanged *Left* and and a modified, less attractive version of *Right*, such as *Right'* $= (45, .25; 10, .75)$. This time *Left* may be preferred which means the higher outcome of *Right* must be improved a little, perhaps to 52.5 or 52 if we do not want to annoy the participant with fractions. Note that we used our good old bisection here – if the participant obeys first-order stochastic dominance, *Left* $= (30, 0.25; 20, 0.75)$ will be preferred over $(30, 0.25; 10, .75)$. Thus 30 is the logical lower bound for the value of s, the better outcome of *Right*. Since 60 (which we tried first) was apparently too high, we then tried 45, the midpoint between 30 and 60, which turned out to be too low. Therefore, we tried 52.5 (the midpoint between 45 and 60) and so on. In a few steps we narrow it down as much as the (typically fuzzy) preference of the participant will allow.

Once indifference is established for some level of s, which we will henceforth call x_1, the weighted utilities of the two gambles must be identical:

$$w^+(p)u(x_0) + (1 - w^+(p))u(R) = w^+(p)u(x_1) + (1 - w^+(p))u(r).$$

Rearranging gives:

$$u(x_1) - u(x_0) = \frac{(u(R) - u(r))(1 - w^+(p))}{w^+(p)}.$$

This is the point where the less trivial adaptive nature of the design kicks in. Once we know x_1, we plug it into the *Left* gamble, instead of x_0. In our example, suppose we found indifference for $s = x_1 = 55$. *Left* will then become $(55, 0.25; 20, 0.75)$ and again we will look for such *Right* $= (t, .25; 10, .75)$ that the two are equally good. Because *Left* is improved, compared to the previous round, so must be *Right*, so we must search for the right t among numbers greater than 55. Once we find it (and, not surprisingly, henceforth start referring to this level of t as x_2), we will get another identity:

$$w^+(p)u(x_1) + (1 - w^+(p))u(R) = w^+(p)u(x_2) + (1 - w^+(p))u(r).$$

Naturally, this yields:

$$u(x_2) - u(x_1) = \frac{(u(R) - u(r))(1 - w^+(p))}{w^+(p)} = u(x_1) - u(x_0),$$

as required, so that a standard sequence x_0, x_1, x_2 has been found. The utility gains corresponding to moving from x_0 to x_1 and from x_1 to x_2 are identical. Because the intercept and the unit of the utility function are arbitrary, we can without loss of generality set $x_0 = 0$ and $x_1 = 1$ which obviously implies $x_2 = 2$. In the same vein, the researcher may find as many additional x_i points equally spaced in terms of utility as she pleases. The initial choice of r, R, and p determines how large the intervals between the x's will be, but they will obviously also depend on the the preference of the participant at hand: for highly concave utility functions and low weights associated with .25, the sequence of x's will rise quickly.

Once such a standard sequence is found, it is also possible to elicit the PWF (Abdellaoui 2000; Bleichrodt and Pinto 2000). The simplest way to proceed is as follows: if we can find the probability q for which obtaining x_1 for sure is as good as obtaining x_2 with probability q and x_0 otherwise, we conclude that $w^+(q) = 0.5$, because it is then true that both yield the weighted utility of 1. If such q is equal to 0.5, we have a case of correct probability weighting; if a higher q is required, it means that undue weight is given to the lower outcome, which would be consistent with a concave PWF corresponding to pessimism. Of course, we cannot be sure that PWF is globally concave, so in any case we would often like to obtain the inverse of the PWF also for values other than 0.5. There are two simple ways to do it. One is to iterate the operation just described. For example, once the value of q we have just characterised (as $q : w^+(q) = .5$) is found, we can find q' such that $(x_1, q; x_0, 1-q)$ and $(x_2, q'; x_0, 1-q')$ are equally good, from which it will follow that $w^+(q') = .25$. The inverse of the PWF at 0.75, and then at 0.125, 0.375, 0.625, and 0.875 can be found in the same way, giving a very good idea of the shape of the PWF, whether it is convex, concave, or inverse-S-shaped or takes yet another shape. Alternatively, we can elicit a longer standard sequence, say of length $k > 2$. Then, finding p_i such that $(x_k, p_i; x_0, 1 - p_i)$ is as good as x_i yields $w^+(p_i)$ for $i = 1, ..., k - 1$. The beauty of such an elicitation procedure is that we need not make any parametric assumptions about the PWF or the utility function (although we may choose a functional form ex post and estimate the parameters). As long as they are both strictly increasing, we will always find appropriate values to establish the equalities we need.

As indicated before, the propagation of error is a serious problem here. If, for some reason, x_2 is overestimated such that $u(x_2) - u(x_1) > u(x_1) - u(x_0)$, then the same is likely to be the case for all the subsequent intervals in the standard sequence. Moreover, the inverse of the PWF cannot then be elicited correctly.

Another undesirable feature of the procedure is that halfway through the experiment, we are switching from finding an *outcome* that would make two gambles equally good to finding a *probability* that would make two gambles equally good. This *scale compatibility* problem (Fox et al. 1998) makes the task harder for the subjects and has been shown to distort choices. The variation of the method used by Bleichrodt and Pinto (2000) evades this problem, although it leads to some other problematic features, as discussed by the authors.

Yet another issue is that eliciting the (inverse of the) PWFs at points that are very close to one another would require either a very long standard sequence or several iterations of bisection. To be fair, for the greatest part of the 0–1 interval on which the PWF is defined, we are usually not very curious about its shape. If, say, by our estimate $w^+(.6) = .5$ and $w^+(.86) = .75$, then, empirically, it is a very good guess that $w^+(.73) = w^+((.6 + .86)/2) = (w^+(.6) + w^+(.86))/2 = (.75 + .5)/2 = .625$, there is thus little need to actually elicit it. That is because in this range, the PWF tends to be nearly linear. This is not so close to the ends of the interval – that is, for unlikely outcomes (that are also extreme, i.e. either the worst or the best, but, naturally, in the most commonly considered case of two-outcome gambles, *all* outcomes are extreme in this sense). Existing literature provides a strong hint that the PWF may be highly non-linear near 0 and 1. In particular, the leading explanation of high demand for lotteries is that the very low probability of winning the jackpot is often highly overweighted, generally meaning that the slope of the PWF at 0 is much higher than just a bit further away from 0, a case of strong local concavity. By the same token, almost-certain gains appear much worse than certain gains, implying that the PWF is much steeper at 1 than it is just a bit further away from 1, a case of strong local convexity.

For this reason, we would like to have a very detailed look at the shape of the PWF very close to the ends of the interval on which it is defined. On top of the difficulties mentioned before, another one arises here, related to the strength of incentives. Suppose the researcher elicits five points equally spaced in terms of utility. Denoting the inverse PWF at a by p_a, such a sequence allows eliciting $p_{1/4}$ in the first step, $p_{1/16}$ in the second step and overall $p_{4^{-i}}$ in ith step. In this procedure, the expected value of the gamble that the subject is asked to consider (to reveal the point of indifference) is four times lower in each step than in the previous step. As a result, either we start with extremely high expected value (EV), or by the time we get to considering really low probabilities that we are interested in, the EV is very low. This makes incentivisation, which is problematic for this procedure anyway (as we will discuss later), even more problematic. Unless we have a huge budget, we cannot truthfully (and credibly) tell subjects that their initial choices (those with very high EV) may be implemented for real. If, by contrast, we start with reasonable EVs and end up with tiny ones, it is hard to see why subjects would care much about these later questions (involving tiny chances for getting moderate amounts of money) even if one of them may be implemented for real.

These considerations motivated the development of the procedure for direct elicitation of a sequence of cumulative probabilities yielding constant decision weights proposed by Krawczyk. This time, the possibility of negative pay-offs is also necessary, which, under CPT are weighted using a separate PWF, w^-. We will also need gambles with three outcomes, one of them being positive, one negative, and one zero. Under CPT, positive and negative outcomes are weighted separately, so obtaining some $GAIN > 0$ with probability p, suffering a $LOSS < 0$ with probability r and obtaining nothing otherwise yields $w^+(p)u(GAIN) + w^-(r)u(LOSS)$. Because we are interested in very low probabilities and, to make them meaningful, very high pay-offs, we may, for example, start with $GAIN = 1,000,000, LOSS = 10, p = p_0 = 0, r = .2$. We also fix $s = .3$, the probability of a loss in an alternative gamble. Now, we seek such q, the probability of $GAIN$ in this alternative gamble, that indifference obtains between the two:

$$w^+(p_0)u(GAIN) + w^-(r)u(LOSS) = w^+(q)u(GAIN) + w^-(s)u(LOSS).$$

Because probability of the loss in the right-hand-side gamble is higher $s = .3 > .2 = r$, to find indifference, so must be the probability of gain ($q > 0$, which is fortunate, because probabilities are rarely below 0). The q for which indifference is established will be denoted by p_1. The reader will not be surprised to hear that this p_1 is subsequently plugged in instead of p_0 in the left-hand-side gamble and the whole operation is iterated. In Krawczyk, it was performed seven times, yielding:

$$u(GAIN)[w^+(p_i) - w^+(p_{i-1})] = u(LOSS)[w^-(r) - w^-(s)],$$

for $i = 1,...,8$. Note that the right-hand side, as well as $u(GAIN)$, is kept unchanged, so that $[w^+(p_i) - w^+(p_{i-1})]$ must also be the same for all the i's, an equivalent of Wakker and Deneffe's standard sequence of outcomes in the probability space:

$$w^+(p_1) - w^+(p_0) = w^+(p_2) - w^+(p_1) = \cdots = w^+(p_8) - w^+(p_7).$$

As we have $p_0 = 0$, this is equivalent to $w^+(p_i)/w^+(p_1) = i$ for $i = 2,...,8$. Now, we do not know the specific value of any $w^+(p_i)$. That would require eventually reaching $p_j = 1$ for some large j (in which case we would know that $w^+(p_j) = 1$ and so would know that $w^+(p_i) = i/j$ for all $i = 1,...j$). This is not feasible, however, because we cannot consider probabilities of the positive outcome higher than $1 - r$ here.

Even if we do not know any of the $w^+(p_i)$s (except, of course, $p_0 = 0$), we can still tell its shape (close to 0). For example $p_1 - p_0 < p_2 - p_1 < \cdots < p_8 - p_7$

would be equivalent to local concavity (changes in probability of gain being less and less important as we move away from 0).

While we focused on the elicitation of the utility function and PWF, similar logic could be applied to other domains in which we are interested in identifying the shape of a function defined on a continuous set, such as in temporal discounting.

5.5 Sequential Designs

In this section, we describe techniques where, given the answers to questions $1, \ldots, k-1$, question k is chosen as the question which will give the most informative answer, based on information already given. While adaptive sequential designs in principle enable more efficient questioning in terms of additional information gained from each question, there is a price to be paid in terms of assumptions. Here, we deal with Bayesian approaches, although it should also be pointed out that the approach of Perny, Viappiani, and Boukhatem (2016) is a good non-Bayesian approach. This is a minimax approach for decision-making under risk with the rank-dependent utility model, which uses linear programming. We focus on the Bayesian approaches (Chapman et al. 2018 and Toubia et al. 2013) while pointing out that there is also extensive work (Cavagnaro et al. 2010) that adopts the Bayesian paradigm. The set-up for utility and decision both for Chapman and colleagues (2018) and Toubia and colleagues (2013) is based on the prospect theory of Tversky and Kahneman; it is necessary to have strong limits on the number of parameters. We'll also see heavy parametric assumptions on likelihood and prior. As we have seen, the expected utilities are non-linear, adding to the computational complexity. The questions are framed such that there is a binary choice (and the possibility of refusing both options is not available). Logistic probability models are used for choosing between the alternatives.

Three variants of this are

- DOSE (Dynamically Optimised Sequential Experimentation) by Chapman and colleagues (2018),
- The approach by Toubia and colleagues (2013),
- ADO (Adaptive Design Optimisation) by Cavagnaro and colleagues (2013).

The 'abstract' is straightforward; assuming we have received (and processed) answers for m questions, question $m + 1$ is chosen to maximise the expected additional information according to a sensible criterion. All three use SIG as presented by Lindley (1956) (and discussed in Section 3.3), where the design is optimal (at least approximately) with SIG utility. While theoretically clear, there are computational difficulties and approximations are required. Chapman and colleagues and Toubia and colleagues take entirely different approaches dealing with this; Chapman and colleagues take a finite discrete set of parameter values and then proceed according to a full Bayesian framework. Their method therefore has all the theoretical guarantees of the Bayesian approach. Toubia, on the other hand, use a truncated normal prior and normal approximations along the way. They make normal approximations along the way, which are necessary to make the problem computationally feasible. These approximations correspond to the 'mean field' approximation of variational Bayes, which provides a lower bound for the log partition function, but there are no theoretical guarantees. The ADO approach, as with DOSE, takes a finite discrete set of parameter values.

Having restricted themselves to a finite discrete parameter space, Chapman and colleagues use Lindley's approach to determine the next question. For Toubia's approach, normal approximations with the same mean and variance structure are used to compute the SIG.

The approach of Toubia and colleagues adds an extra layer for the prior and this has room for development; there is a first-stage prior over the parameter vectors for the subjects and there is a second-stage prior over the parameters of the first-stage prior. The parameter vectors for each subject are considered to be conditionally independent, conditioned on the first-stage prior parameters (so that the set-up has similarities to the move from multinomial logit to the RPM).

In a situation where subjects can be clustered and the first-stage prior parameters are similar within a cluster (and markedly different between clusters), it is straightforward to extend the approach of Toubia and colleagues by setting up a suitable prior for assigning subjects to clusters. The first stage prior parameters are drawn from the second stage prior, independently for each cluster.

We start with a *utility function* for the subject, with some unknown parameters. Based on the utility, we also have an *expected utility* (computed by averaging the utility over the possible outcomes that may result from a decision, according to their probabilities). The expected utility can include additional unknown parameters – for example, the probability weights for the possible outcomes of a decision could depend on a latent class variable. We place a prior over these parameters and/or models and, based on that prior, select the question that will give the most informative answer. After the answer is obtained, the prior is updated to the posterior, the posterior is then the 'new' prior, which is used to determine the next question, and so on. The sequence continues in this way until either the participant has been asked the preset number of questions, or the precision of the estimates (based on the current posterior) for that participant is greater than some pre-specified criterion (or none of the possible questions that can be posed are sufficiently informative according to, e.g., the SIG criterion).

There is a *consistency parameter* which accommodates the fact that subjects may give wrong answers that do not correspond to their expected utility. For an RUM, this is the parameter which governs the error component. By including all these parameters and placing an appropriate prior over them, we can accommodate the fact that the participant may give some wrong answers; by suitable choice of prior, if most of the answers are correct, the procedure will still update to a posterior over the parameter space that gives a good assessment of the correct parameters. In this sense, there are similarities, at least in spirit, with the approach of Toubia, Hauser, and Garcia (2007) to conjoint analysis where the possibility of errors is accounted for and hence a useful posterior is obtained even if some of the answers are incorrect.

5.5.1 Errors and Choice Consistency

We assume that an individual has a *utility function* $u(x;\zeta)$, taking the sum of money x and vector of individual characteristics ζ as arguments.

We also let α denote the additional parameters required to define the *expected utility* and $w = (\zeta, \alpha)$. The expected utility is then:

$$V(a|w) = \mathbb{E}_a^{\alpha}[u(X|\zeta)] = \sum_i q_i u(x_i|\zeta),$$

where the sum is over the possible outcomes when decision a is taken, (x_i) denotes the possible outcomes and the (q_i)'s are the prospect theory *probability weights*; q_i the probability weight assigned to outcome i. Depending on the PWF (for gains and losses) explored before, the q_is are not necessarily equal to the probability p_i of outcome i; the parameters α parametrise the PWF.

Example 5.1 Consider a simple example where there are two options: the first (which we denote a_1) is to do nothing and receive €15, while the second (denoted by a_2) is to pay €10 to enter a lottery, where the payout is either €0 or €50, each with probability $\frac{1}{2}$. Suppose that $\mathbb{E}_a^{\alpha}$ denotes a simple expectation (no distortion; $q_i = p_i$), then:

$$V(a_1|\zeta) = u(15|\zeta) \qquad V(a_2|\zeta) = \frac{1}{2}u(-10|\zeta) + \frac{1}{2}u(40|\zeta)$$

(bearing in mind that the second option involved buying a lottery ticket which cost €10). □

Suppose a question has q possible responses, say $a_1, \ldots, a_q$ (rather than two, a_1 and a_2, as in the example). Let A denote the choice set: $A = \{a_1, \ldots, a_q\}$. One possibility for the probability distribution over A is:

$$\mathbb{P}(a|w) = \frac{e^{\nu V(a|\zeta)}}{\sum_{b \in A} e^{\nu V(b|\zeta)}} \qquad a \in A. \tag{5.1}$$

This is basically a multinomial logit. Both Chapman and colleagues and Toubia and colleagues restrict to binary choices and use this probability, with an appropriate definition of V. The important point here is the parameter ν, the *consistency parameter*. The larger the value of ν, the greater the probability that the subject will choose the decision that gives the maximum value for V.

Toubia and colleagues restrict the discussion to the situation where:

- For each question, the subject has to decide between two options and
- Each option has two possible outcomes.

We follow this because it makes the notation easier, but the general idea can be extended quite easily.

5.5.2 Probability Weighting and Time Discounting

Both Chapman and colleagues (2018) and Toubia and colleagues (2013) investigate a hypothesis central in behavioural economics, that people treat losses and gains differently, where utility functions are motivated by prospect theory; for the risk preference study, the two-parameter utility function,

$$u(x; \rho, \lambda) = x^{\rho} \mathbf{1}_{[0,+\infty)}(x) - \lambda(-x)^{\rho} \mathbf{1}_{(-\infty,0)}(x), \tag{5.2}$$

is used, where $\lambda \in \mathbb{R}_+$ describes *loss aversion*, while the parameter $\rho \in \mathbb{R}_+$ describes *risk aversion* and $x \in \mathbb{R}$ is the amount of money relative to the reference point. If $\lambda > 1$, then the participant takes negative outcomes more seriously, while for $\lambda < 1$, the participant takes negative outcomes (with respect to the reference point) less seriously. If the PWF is the identity function, then a value of $\rho < 1$ shows risk aversion, while $\rho = 1$ means no risk aversion.

The two-parameter utility function (5.2) has the minimum number of parameters necessary to model both these points; risk aversion/tolerance modelled by ρ, relative importance of gains versus losses modelled by λ. For parameter estimation, the fewer parameters that reasonably describe the picture, the better.

Toubia and colleagues (2013) include the *distortion of probability* modelled using the PWF $w^{\pm}(p)$ which we will simply denote $w(p)$ (since we take $w^+ = w^- = w$). In Toubia, this is:

$$w(p) = \exp\{-(-\log p)^{\alpha}\}.$$

The distortion is modelled by a single parameter α. If $\alpha = 1$, then $w(p) = p$. For all $\alpha > 0$, the function $w(p)$ satisfies $w(0) = 0$, $w(1) = 1$ as it should. For $p < e^{-1}$, we have $w(p) > p$ for $\alpha \in (0,1)$ and $w(p) < p$ for $\alpha > 1$, so that, for $\alpha \in (0,1)$, the distortion magnifies small probabilities. Again, we denote option a by the quadruple $(x, p; y, 1-p)$, where the notation means that the outcome is x with probability p and y with probability $1-p$. The function V is then defined as:

$$V(x,p;y,1-p) = \begin{cases} w(p)u(x) + (1 - w(p))u(y) & x > y > 0 \quad \text{or} \quad x < y < 0, \\ w(p)u(x) + w(1-p)u(y) & x < 0 < y \end{cases}$$

where the values are ordered such that $|x| > |y|$. In Chapman and colleagues the PWF is not included; $w(p) = p$.

Time Preference Utility For *time preference*, Chapman and colleagues add a parameter to Equation (5.2) to accommodate *time discounting*. If an amount x is to be paid at payment time t, the utility function may be written as:

$$u(t,x|\rho,\lambda,r) = e^{-rt}(x^{\rho}\mathbf{1}_{[0,+\infty)}(x) - \lambda(-x)^{\rho}\mathbf{1}_{(-\infty,0)}(x)). \tag{5.3}$$

The parameter r enables comparison between pay-off now (time 0) and a given time later (time t). Chapman and colleagues only consider *one* fixed time t in the future. Toubia and colleagues consider a time-preference utility function of:

$$u(t,x|r,\beta) = x\left(\mathbf{1}_{\{t=0\}} + \beta e^{-rt}\mathbf{1}_{(0,+\infty)}(t)\right) = V(t,x|r,\beta). \tag{5.4}$$

The β parameter of Toubia and colleagues models *present bias*, a sudden difference between obtaining payment now and any time in the future. This can easily be added to the risk-time preference utility of (5.3) at the expense of an additional parameter:

$$\begin{cases} u(t,x|\rho,\lambda,\beta,r) = \delta(t)\left(x^{\rho}\mathbf{1}_{[0,+\infty)}(x) - \lambda(-x)^{\rho}\mathbf{1}_{(-\infty,0)}(x)\right) \\ \delta(t) = \mathbf{1}_{\{t=0\}} + \beta e^{-rt}\mathbf{1}_{(0,+\infty)}(t) \end{cases}. \tag{5.5}$$

These utility functions encapsulate risk preference/aversion and loss preference/aversion, and the modification from (5.2) to (5.3) and (5.5) also encapsulates time preferences. The problem here is that they are not conducive to likelihoods which update a prior to a posterior within a conjugate family that is computationally convenient.

5.5.3 Implementation

The solution adopted by Chapman and colleagues (2018) is to map out all possible sets of binary choices in advance; the tree is then used to route the respondents through the survey. Mapping such a tree with a prior over a large set of possible values is infeasible, hence a subset is chosen to make this computationally feasible. After the responses are obtained, they may then be processed using the full prior. The main outstanding question here (of course) is where to get these parameter values from. These come from previous studies of prospect theory utility functions and their parameter estimates. Chapman and colleagues applied DOSE for a large survey of the US population which studied risk preferences and time preferences; the choice of parameters followed *previous* participant estimates studying similar questions, taken from Sokol-Hessner and colleagues (2009) and Frydman and colleagues (2011).

Simulation Studies Chapman and colleagues tested the method using simulation, using data from previous laboratory experiments. In each experiment, participants were given the same set of 140 binary choices. The order of the questions in the experiments was random, while in the simulation, the questions were ordered optimally for each participant using DOSE. After DOSE selected a question, it was provided with the answer the participant gave in the experiment. The procedure then updated the probability distribution over parameters, selected the next question, and so on. At each stage, the inaccuracy of the DOSE estimate was computed in terms of the absolute distance of the maximum a posteriori probability estimate (MAP) - that is, the value that maximises the posterior - from the true parameter value as a percentage of the true value. The *true* parameter values are (of course) not available, hence those obtained using choices from all 140 questions are used; the aim is to see whether DOSE answers using fewer questions are close to these.

Simulation studies showed that a 20-question DOSE sequence provided a similar amount of information as approximately 50 randomly ordered questions.

Survey of Risk and Time Preference The survey of Chapman and colleagues included two DOSE survey modules, the first focusing on risk preferences and the second on time preferences. The first consisted of ten binary choices between a fixed certain amount and a lottery. The second consisted of a further ten binary choices between differing amounts at two different dates. The questions were designed to provide information about all the parameters of interest. The risk module was executed first and information was carried over to the time module. For risk, the first four questions were restricted to lotteries over *gains* so that precise information about ρ could be established before moving onto λ.

The survey was implemented using YouGov's online platform, where choosing questions in real time was not possible. Instead, all possible sets of binary choices were mapped out in advance on a binary tree. This binary tree was then used to route respondents through the survey. The data was analysed using a 100-point discretised prior, but mapping such a tree with the 100-point discretised parameter space was not possible, because of computational constraints and also the limitations of YouGov's interface; such a tree mapped over 20 questions would require more than 500,000 routes through the survey.

Therefore, a smaller number of possible parameter values was used to create the binary tree and decide on the sequence of questions; the data was then reanalysed ex post with the 100-point discretised parameter space. The risk-preference values for the utility function were used for the time-preference study; respondents were each assigned to one of ten prior distributions over ρ, the risk preference/aversion parameter, based on their estimated value of ρ from the risk-loss experiment.

Chapman and colleagues (2018) used an *incentivised* representative survey of the US population with 2,000 subjects to estimate risk and time preferences; they were particularly interested in loss aversion, modelled by the λ parameter in the risk preference and time preference utility functions (5.2) and (5.3). It was comprehensive, using a wide range of elicitations to measure different preferences and was repeated (i.e. the same participants are asked the same questions) six months apart. The behavioural measures were all incentivised by selecting two of the survey modules at random for payment at the end of the survey.

All outcomes were expressed in YouGov points, an internal YouGov currency used to pay panel members, which can be converted to US dollars using the approximate rate of $0.001 per point. To enhance the credibility of these incentives, the sample was restricted to those who had already been paid (in cash or prizes) for their participation in surveys. The average payment to respondents (including the show-up fee) was $9 (9,000 points), which was approximately three times the average for YouGov surveys.

5.5.4 Remarks

1. Chapman and colleagues and Toubia and colleagues both deal with the same problem, Chapman approximating by taking a finite discrete

parameter space, Toubia retaining the continuous state space, but essentially using Gaussian approximations.

The class of problems has strong similarities to 'classification and regression trees', where the parameter is the 'class' variable (in the discretise setting of Chapman et al.) or the 'regressor' (in the continuous setting of Toubia et al.). This class of techniques has wide applications; the problem we have here is to balance the use of simplifying approximations to make the problem computationally feasible with required accuracy.

2. As we have seen, the DOSE procedure requires a discretisation and only a few possible parameter choices can be considered. The approach by Toubia and colleagues allows for continuous distributions, but uses Gaussian approximations at several stages to make it computationally feasible.
3. These approximations (Chapman et al. discretise the parameter space, while Toubia et al. take continuous parameter space, but use normal approximations) seem necessary to produce the next question in real time. In both, there is a 'rough' procedure that can be performed in real time for choosing questions and then a more rigorous procedure for analysing the data once all the answers have been obtained.
4. An important issue is the choice of priors; Chapman and colleagues chose their discretised parameter space and the prior distribution over it from earlier studies, Sokol-Hessner and colleagues (2009) and Frydman and colleagues (2011).
5. Chapman and colleagues carried out simulations which showed that a twenty-question DOSE sequence, using the 'rough' discretisation, provided a similar amount of information as approximately fifty randomly ordered questions. The extent to which a finer discretisation might lead to a further reduction in the number of questions required to provide similar information to fifty randomly ordered questions was not discussed. This would (of course) slow down the computation of the next question. The reduction from fifty to twenty already represents a substantial improvement.

5.6 Incentivising Dynamic Designs

We now consider the problem of *incentivising* dynamic designs, so that subjects have a reason to give truthful answers.

As pointed out earlier, Chapman and colleagues (2018) incentivised their experiment by, at the end of the experiment, randomly selecting two of the modules for payment. This corresponds to the random lottery incentive systems typically used in static designs (whereby one or more of the choices made by the subject are chosen at random and implemented). This could be problematic for an adaptive design, because the participants could, in principle, make choices which are inconsistent with their preferences, with a view to yielding them better options to choose from in subsequent questions, thus increasing their expected pay-off. For example, when we elicit a standard sequence as discussed before, once x_1 is plugged into the *Left* gamble, participants may guess that it is in their interest that x_2 is as high as possible because it will be featured in future options. They may thus keep saying that they prefer *Left* to get a really good deal in subsequent questions. Telling participants in such a case that it is actually in their best interest to choose the preferred option in each choice is widely considered to be deceptive, both by experimentalists and participants (Kachurka et al. 2021). One could thus consider one of several alternative ways to incentivise dynamic designs.

One way is that the experimenter chooses at random one of many choice situations that the subject *could* get. If this real choice situation (RCS) (the term used by Johnson et al. 2021) already appears in the set optimally chosen for a given subject, then implement it. If RCS does not appear in the sequence, then assign one of the options of the RCS at random. The problem with this approach is that the incentive could be very weak since, given the large number of *possible* questions, the chance that the subject is actually asked the question selected for reward is very small. If there are (say) 100,000 possible choice situations and the subject is only exposed to (say) 10, then there is only a chance of 1 in 10,000 that any answer matters, so that, for practical purposes, there are no incentives.

Another method is to simply add an RCS to the otherwise optimal set of questions. An extra question should not be very different from other questions. If all but one of the questions are about millions of dollars, it will be easy to guess that the odd one is to be implemented (and, for obvious reasons, we normally *do not* want extremely high payments featured in the RCS). Appending a predetermined RCS may also be difficult in adaptive designs where successive questions refine the preference range, so that there is an internal logic to the sequence; in such a case, it may be clear to the subject which question is the artificially added RCS. A fine point concerns avoiding deception if such a procedure is used. Researchers should not claim that RCS is picked at random (because it is not). By contrast, a statement along the lines of 'one of the choices will be implemented and you cannot tell which one this would be' should in principle have analogous incentivising effects.

These two methods can be combined: we can use our target RCS if it appears in the sequence that the subject saw and append it at the end of this sequence otherwise. Again, a very malicious referee could claim that this is a subtle form of deception because we tell the participant that any of their choices can matter while knowing it is extremely unlikely that any of the choices, except for the last one, will matter.

Another mechanism trying to take the best of two worlds is PRINCE by Johnson and colleagues (2021). These authors also propose that the RCS be placed in a sealed envelope before the experiment so that it is transparent that it is predetermined (and so it is indeed optimal to truthfully report the preferred option in each question which may just turn out to be the RCS). It is not obvious how to implement it in an online experiment. A password-protected file that the participant stores on their disc prior to the experiment, but is only able to open after the experiment, could possibly serve as a virtual equivalent of a sealed envelope (although most users have a reasonable aversion to downloading unusual files). The authors also suggest, and we believe they are right, that transparency of incentive compatibility may be improved by making it easy for the participants to record their own choices.[1]

An alternative approach would then be to *estimate* the utility function and apply it to an exogenously chosen choice situation (Ding 2007). After answering the sequence of choice questions, the subject is presented with another exogenous choice situation, but not asked to state a preference; instead, the subject's preferred option is inferred from the answers to previous choice questions and implemented. It is therefore in the subject's best interest to help the experimenter estimate the subject's preference correctly.

One problem may be that the experimenter gets the preference of the subject wrong, perhaps due to errors made by the subject in some of the answers. If I participate in an experiment and come to a conclusion that inference along the lines of 'based on your previous answers, we believe that out of these two options you prefer X over Y' is blatantly incorrect, it can have a demoralising effect. Indeed, it makes the researchers look incompetent *and* malicious – if they wanted to know if I preferred X over Y they should have asked me! A softer version of this mechanism could thus be considered in which the subject has an option to revert to the inferred choice, but (to keep incentives in place) at a price. Of course, this makes the procedure yet more complex. In either

[1] Johnson and colleagues (2021) also insist that participants should be asked to give experimenters 'instructions' as to which option from the RCS should be implemented. Perhaps we are overly conservative and used to the traditional direction of instructions in experiments – from experimenter to participants – but it seems to us that it is yet to be demonstrated that such a framing improves transparency (and, as a result, e.g., reduces share of choices that are obviously inconsistent with preferences). In particular, formulating the BDM mechanism in terms of participants giving 'instructions' does not seem to solve the problems which we discussed earlier, described in Horowitz (2006), because the basic gamble taken by the subject when stating the WTP threshold is the same.

version, the scheme is not transparent to the subjects: because estimation of preference is far from trivial, they cannot verify if and how their choices really matter. Then again, in the times of Amazon and Netflix and a hundred other services using mysterious algorithms to make recommendations based on our previous choices, this may be a situation to which most of us are well used. In the end, there are no one-size-fits-all solutions and the optimal approach to the trade-off between simplicity, transparency, and strength of incentives may depend on the design and sample at hand.

In any case, as in almost any experiment, participants' trust is a precious resource without which whole volumes devoted to efficient design of experiments may not help much.

References

Abdellaoui, Mohammed. Parameter-free elicitation of utility and probability weighting functions. *Management Science*, 46(11):1497–1512, 2000.

Abdi, Hervé. Bonferroni and Šidák corrections for multiple comparisons. *Encyclopedia of Measurement and Statistics*, 3:103–107, 2007.

Agranov, Marina, Andrew Caplin, and Chloe Tergiman. Naive play and the process of choice in guessing games. *Journal of the Economic Science Association*, 1:146–157, 2015.

Agresti, Alan. *Categorical data analysis*, volume 792. John Wiley & Sons, 2012.

Akaichi, Faical, Joan Costa-Font, and Richard Frank. Uninsured by choice? A choice experiment on long term care insurance. *Journal of Economic Behavior & Organization*, 173:422–434, 2020.

Andreoni, James. Why free ride? Strategies and learning in public goods experiments. *Journal of Public Economics*, 37(3):291–304, 1988.

Bleichrodt, Han, and Jose Luis Pinto. A parameter-free elicitation of the probability weighting function in medical decision analysis. *Management Science*, 46(11):1485–1496, 2000.

Box, E. P. George, William Gordon Hunter, and J. Stuart Hunter. *Statistics for experimenters: Design, innovation, and discovery*, 2nd edition. Wiley, 2005.

Brady, Henry E. Causation and explanation in social science. In Robert E. Goodin, editor, *The Oxford handbook of political science*, Oxford University Press, 2008.

Bucknell, John, Justin S. White, and Ce Shang. Can incentive-compatibility reduce hypothetical bias in smokers' experimental choice behavior? A randomized discrete choice experiment. *Journal of Choice Modelling*, 37:100255, 2020.

Cavagnaro, Daniel R., Richard Gonzalez, Jay I. Myung, and Mark A. Pitt. Optimal decision stimuli for risky choice experiments: An adaptive approach. *Management Science*, 59(2):358–375, 2013.

Cavagnaro, Daniel R., Jay I. Myung, Mark A. Pitt, and Janne V. Kujala. Adaptive design optimization: A mutual information-based approach to model discrimination in cognitive science. *Neural Computation*, 22(4):887–905, 2010.

Cetre, Sophie, Max Lobeck, Claudia Senik, and Thierry Verdier. Preferences over income distribution: Evidence from a choice experiment. *Journal of Economic Psychology*, 74:102202, 2019.

Chapman, Jonathan, Erik Snowberg, Stephanie Wang, and Colin Camerer. Loss attitudes in the U.S. population: Evidence from Dynamically Optimized Sequential Experimentation (DOSE). Technical report, National Bureau of Economic Research, 2018.

Charness, Gary, Uri Gneezy, and Michael A. Kuhn. Experimental methods: Between-subject and within-subject design. *Journal of Economic Behavior & Organization*, 81(1):1–8, 2012.

Clark, Andrew E., Claudia Senik, and Katsunori Yamada. When experienced and decision utility concur: The case of income comparisons. *Journal of Behavioral and Experimental Economics*, 70:1–9, 2017.

Croissant, Yves. Estimation of random utility models in r: The mlogit package. *Journal of Statistical Software*, 95(11):1–41, 2020. https://doi.org/10.18637/jss.v095.i11.

Czajkowski, Mikolaj, Marek Giergiczny, and William H. Greene. Learning and fatigue effects revisited: Investigating the effects of accounting for unobservable preference and scale heterogeneity. *Land Economics*, 90(2):324–351, 2014.

Ding, Min. An incentive-aligned mechanism for conjoint analysis. *Journal of Marketing Research*, 44(2):214–223, 2007.

Fox, Armando, Steven D. Gribble, Yatin Chawathe, and Eric A. Brewer. Adapting to network and client variation using infrastructural proxies: Lessons and perspectives. *IEEE Personal Communications*, 5(4):10–19, 1998.

Frydman, Cary, Colin Camerer, Peter Bossaerts, and Antonio Rangel. Maoa-l carriers are better at making optimal financial decisions under risk. *Proceedings of the Royal Society B: Biological Sciences*, 278(1714):2053–2059, 2011.

Harrison, Glenn W., Morten I. Lau, and E. Elisabet Rutström. Risk attitudes, randomization to treatment, and self-selection into experiments. *Journal of Economic Behavior & Organization*, 70(3):498–507, 2009.

Hess, Stephane, and David Palma. Apollo: A flexible, powerful and customisable freeware package for choice model estimation and application. *Journal of Choice Modelling*, 32:100170, 2019.

Holland, Paul W. Causation and race. *ETS Research Report Series*, 2003(1): i–21, 2003.

Holland, Paul W. Statistics and causal inference. *Journal of the American Statistical Association*, 81(396):945–960, 1986.

Horiuchi, Yusaku, Zachary Markovich, and Teppei Yamamoto. Does conjoint analysis mitigate social desirability bias? *Political Analysis*, 30(4):535–549, 2022.

Horowitz, John K. The Becker–DeGroot–Marschak mechanism is not necessarily incentive compatible, even for non-random goods. *Economics Letters*, 93(1):6–11, 2006.

Jacquemet, Nicolas, and Olivier l'Haridon. *Experimental economics*. Cambridge University Press, 2018.

Johnson, Cathleen, Aurélien Baillon, Han Bleichrodt, Zhihua Li, Dennie Van Dolder, and Peter P. Wakker. PRINCE: An improved method for measuring incentivized preferences. *Journal of Risk and Uncertainty*, 62(1):1–28, 2021.

Kachurka, Raman, Michał Krawczyk, and Joanna Rachubik. State lottery in the lab: an experiment in external validity. *Experimental Economics*, 24: 1242–1266, 2021.

Krawczyk, Michał. What should be regarded as deception in experimental economics? Evidence from a survey of researchers and subjects. *Journal of Behavioral and Experimental Economics*, 79:110–118, 2019.

Krawczyk, Michał, Andrea Blasco, Tomasz Gajderowicz, and Marek Giergiczny. Europeans' attitudes towards displaced populations: Evidence from a conjoint experiment on support for temporary protection, 2023. Available at https://ssrn.com/abstract=4564737 or http://dx.doi.org/10.2139/ssrn.4564737.

Krawczyk, Michał, and Marta Sylwestrzak. Exploring the role of deliberation time in non-selfish behavior: The double response method. *Journal of Behavioral and Experimental Economics*, 72:121–134, 2018.

Levitt, Steven D., and John A. List. Field experiments in economics: The past, the present, and the future. *European Economic Review*, 53(1):1–18, 2009.

Lindley, Dennis V. On a measure of the information provided by an experiment. *The Annals of Mathematical Statistics*, 27(4):986–1005, 1956.

List, John. Sometimes winning means knowing when to quit. *Wall Street Journal*, 30 December 2021.

Mahoney, James, and Laura Acosta. A regularity theory of causality for the social sciences. *Quality & Quantity*, 56:1889–1911, 2021.

Mariel, Petr, David Hoyos, Jürgen Meyerhoff, Mikolaj Czajkowski, Thijs Dekker, Klaus Glenk, Jette Bredahl Jacobsen, Ulf Liebe, Søren Bøye Olsen, Julian Sagebiel, and Mara Thiene. *Environmental valuation with discrete choice experiments: Guidance on design, implementation and data analysis*. Springer Nature, 2021.

Marks, David F., and John Colwell. The psychic staring effect. *Skeptical Inquirer*, 24(5):41–49, 2000.

McFadden, Daniel. The measurement of urban travel demand. *Journal of Public Economics*, 3(4):303–328, 1974.

McFadden, Daniel. Modeling the choice of residential location. In Anders Karlqvist, Folke Snickars, and Jürgen Weibull, editors, *Spatial interaction theory and planning models*, pp. 75–96. North Holland, 1978.

Menapace, Luisa, and Roberta Raffaelli. Unraveling hypothetical bias in discrete choice experiments. *Journal of Economic Behavior & Organization*, 176:416–430, 2020.

Meyerhoff, Jürgen, Malte Oehlmann, and Priska Weller. The influence of design dimensions on stated choices in an environmental context. *Environmental and Resource Economics*, 61(3):385–407, 2015.

Moffatt, Peter G. *Experimetrics: Econometrics for experimental economics*. Macmillan International Higher Education, 2015.

Overstall, Antony M., and David C. Woods. Bayesian design of experiments using approximate coordinate exchange. *Technometrics*, 59(4):458–470, 2017.

Papoutsi, Georgia S., Rodolfo M. Nayga Jr, Panagiotis Lazaridis, and Andreas C. Drichoutis. Fat tax, subsidy or both? The role of information and children's pester power in food choice. *Journal of Economic Behavior & Organization*, 117:196–208, 2015.

Pearl, Judea. *Causality*. Cambridge University Press, 2009.

Perny, Patrice, Paolo Viappiani, and Abdellah Boukhatem. Incremental preference elicitation for decision making under risk with the rank-dependent utility model. In Alexander Ihler and Dominik Janzing, editors, *Uncertainty in artificial intelligence*, pp. 597–606. AUAI Press for Association for Uncertainty in Artificial Intelligence, 2016.

Shannon, Claude Elwood. A mathematical theory of communication. *The Bell System Technical Journal*, 27(3):379–423, 1948.

Shigeoka, Hitoshi, and Katsunori Yamada. Income-comparison attitudes in the United States and the United Kingdom: Evidence from discrete-choice experiments. *Journal of Economic Behavior & Organization*, 164:414–438, 2019.

Smith, Mike D. Biased coin randomization. In Narayanaswamy Balakrishnan, editor, *Methods and applications of statistics in clinical trials. Volume 1: Concepts, principles, trials, and design*, pp. 90–105. Wiley, 2014.

Sokol-Hessner, Peter, Ming Hsu, Nina G. Curley, Mauricio R. Delgado, Colin F. Camerer, and Elizabeth A. Phelps. Thinking like a trader selectively reduces individuals' loss aversion. *Proceedings of the National Academy of Sciences*, 106(13):5035–5040, 2009.

Spirtes, Peter, Clark Glymour, and Richard Scheines, with additional material by David Heckerman. *Causation, prediction, and search*. MIT Press, 2001.

Steimle, Lauren N., Yuming Sun, Lauren Johnson, Tibor Besedeš, Patricia Mokhtarian, and Dima Nazzal. Students' preferences for returning to colleges and universities during the COVID-19 pandemic: A discrete choice experiment. *Socio-economic Planning Sciences*, page 101266, 2022.

Student. Appendix to Mercer and Hall's paper 'The experimental error of field trials'. *Journal of Agricultural Science*, 4, 128–131.

Subroy, Vandana, Abbie A. Rogers, and Marit E. Kragt. To bait or not to bait: A discrete choice experiment on public preferences for native wildlife and conservation management in Western Australia. *Ecological Economics*, 147:114–122, 2018.

Thye, Shane. Logical and philosophical foundations of experimental research in the social sciences. In Murray Webster and Jane Sell, editors, *Laboratory experiments in the social sciences*, pp. 53–82. Elsevier, 2014.

Titchener, Edward Bradford. Experimental psychology: A retrospect. *American Journal of Psychology*, 36(3):313–323, 1925.

Toubia, Olivier, John Hauser, and Rosanna Garcia. Probabilistic polyhedral methods for adaptive choice-based conjoint analysis: Theory and application. *Marketing Science*, 26(5):596–610, 2007.

Toubia, Olivier, Eric Johnson, Theodoros Evgeniou, and Philippe Delquié. Dynamic experiments for estimating preferences: An adaptive method of eliciting time and risk parameters. *Management Science*, 59(3):613–640, 2013.

Train, Kenneth E. Recreation demand models with taste differences over people. *Land economics*, University of Wisconsin Press, 74(2), 230–239, 1998.

Tversky, Amos, and Daniel Kahneman. Advances in prospect theory: Cumulative representation of uncertainty. *Journal of Risk and Uncertainty*, 5(4):297–323, 1992.

Tversky, Amos, and Richard H. Thaler. Anomalies: Preference reversals. *Journal of Economic Perspectives*, 4(2):201–211, 1990.

Vossler, Christian A., Maurice Doyon, and Daniel Rondeau. Truth in consequentiality: Theory and field evidence on discrete choice experiments. *American Economic Journal: Microeconomics*, 4(4):145–171, 2012.

Vossler, Christian A., and Mary F. Evans. Bridging the gap between the field and the lab: Environmental goods, policy maker input, and consequentiality. *Journal of Environmental Economics and Management*, 58(3):338–345, 2009.

Wakker, Peter, and Daniel Deneffe. Eliciting von Neumann–Morgenstern utilities when probabilities are distorted or unknown. *Management Science*, 42(8):1131–1150, 1996.

Woodward, James. Causation and manipulability. In Edward N. Zalta, editor, *The Stanford Encyclopedia of Philosophy*. Metaphysics Research Lab, Stanford University, Winter edition, 2016.

Ziliak, Stephen T. Field balanced versus randomized field experiments in economics: Why W. S. Gosset aka 'Student' matters. *Review of Behavioral Economics*, 1(1–2):167–208.

Cambridge Elements

Behavioural and Experimental Economics

Nicolas Jacquemet

University Paris-1 Panthéon Sorbonne and the Paris School of Economics

Nicolas Jacquemet is a full professor at University Paris-1 Panthéon Sorbonne and the Paris School of Economics. His research combines experimental methods and econometrics to study discrimination, the effect of personality traits on economic behaviour, the role of social pre-involvement in strategic behaviour and experimental game theory. His research has been published in *Econometrica*, *Management Science*, *Games and Economic Behavior*, the *Journal of Environmental Economics and Management*, the *Journal of Health Economics*, and the *Journal of Economic Psychology*.

Olivier L'Haridon

Université de Rennes 1

Olivier L'Haridon is a full professor at the Université de Rennes I, France. His research combines experimental methods and decision theory, applied in the study of individual decision making as affected by uncertainty. His work has been published in *American Economic Review*, *Management Science*, the *Journal of Risk and Uncertainty*, *Theory and Decision*, *Experimental Economics*, the *Journal of Health Economics*, and the *Journal of Economic Psychology*.

About the Series

Cambridge Elements in Behavioural and Experimental Economics focuses on recent advances in two of the most important and innovative fields in modern economics. It aims to provide better understanding of economic behavior, choices, strategies and judgements, particularly through the design and use of laboratory experiments.

Cambridge Elements

Behavioural and Experimental Economics

Elements in the Series

Public Finance with Behavioural Agents
Raphaël Lardeux

Estimation of Structural Models Using Experimental Data From the Lab and the Field
Charles Bellemare

Imperfect Perception and Stochastic Choice in Experiments
Pablo Brañas-Garza and John Smith

Advances in Efficient Design of Experiments in Economics
Michał Wiktor Krawczyk and John Masson Noble

A full series listing is available at: www.cambridge.org/BEE

Printed in the United States
by Baker & Taylor Publisher Services